2/01

1 10/05 (5/07)

THE SECRET WAR

WORLD ESPIONAGE

THE SECRET WAR
Espionage in World War II

James T. Rogers

Facts On File
New York • Oxford

The Secret War: Espionage in World War II

Copyright © 1991 by James T. Rogers

Facts On File, Inc.   Facts On File Limited
460 Park Avenue South   Collins Street
New York NY 10016   Oxford 0X4 1XJ
USA   United Kingdom

Library of Congress Cataloging-in-Publication Data
Rogers, James T.
    The secret war : espionage in World War II / James T. Rogers.
        p. cm. — (world espionage)
    Includes bibliographical references and index.
    Summary: Focuses on British and American espionage,
counterespionage, and deceptive operations that were so crucial to
the defeat of Nazi Germany and Japan in the Second World War.
    ISBN 0-8160-2395-6 (alk. paper)
    1. World War, 1939-1945—Secret service—Juvenile literature.
    2. Espionage—History—20th century—Juvenile literature.
    [1. World War, 1939-1945—Secret service. 2. Espionage—
History—20th century.] I. Title. II. Series: Yost, Graham.
World espionage.
    D810.S7R54 1991   91-2724
    940.54′85—dc20

British CIP data available on request from Facts On File.

Jacket design by Catherine Hyman
Composition by Facts On File, Inc.
Manufactured by R.R. Donnelley & Sons
Printed in the United States of America

10 9 8 7 6 5 4 3 2 1

This book is printed on acid-free paper.

CONTENTS

To the men
of the 953rd Field Artillery Battalion
First U.S. Army
European Theater of Operations, 1943–1945

INTRODUCTION
World War II: The Secret Part and the Public Part

To the British his code name was GARBO; to the Germans it was ARABEL. (His real name may have been Felipe Fernandez, or perhaps Luis Calvo or Juan Pujol, but that is a shadowy matter like so much else in the realm of espionage. In any case he was a Spanish journalist before he got into spying.) The Germans regarded him as one of their best spies in England, valuing his work so highly that toward the end of the war they awarded him the Iron Cross. The British knew better. He was in fact a double agent, working for the British while seeming to be working for the Germans. In that role he gave the Germans information the British wanted them to have. He was so successful at it that toward the end of the war the British gave him the MBE (Member of the British Empire), an award for civilians who have rendered outstanding service to the country.

GARBO was a fighter in the secret war—the war of espionage, counterespionage and deception that was almost as crucial a factor in World War II as the armies, navies and air forces were. Reading now the records of the secret war, one is led to the firm conclusion that the British and the Americans were much more successful at it than the Germans and the Japanese were. The main reason was Ultra, the operation in England and the United States by which the British and the Americans broke the codes the Germans and the Japanese used for the many messages they sent by radio. As a result, the Allies obtained vital information, giving them almost throughout the war a clear picture of what the enemy was up to. No other warring nations have enjoyed anything quite like this periscopic view into the enemy camp.

The strange thing is that neither the Germans nor the Japanese ever caught on. They had their suspicions, but in every case they fell back on the belief that their codes were impenetrable. The other side of the coin is the extraordinary effort the Americans and the British put into keeping Ultra secret. Indeed, Ultra remained a secret until 1974, almost 30 years after the end of the war. One result of this intense secrecy is that anything written about the war before 1974 tends to make the Allied generals, admirals and strategists look more brilliant than they were, since it appears that their uncanny ability to have their forces in the right place at the right time so often was due to cleverness and experience rather than foreknowledge.

Ultra was an espionage operation, however much it differed from the traditional picture of the spy lurking in a seamen's tavern picking up naval gossip from the sailors and sending off his reports in secret writing. The work of GARBO and other double agents comes under the heading of counterespionage. At times it involved the third element of the secret war, deception.

Espionage is the effort, usually carried out in secret, to discover things the enemy is trying to keep secret. What is the strength of its forces? Where are its troops, ships and planes? How strong is its production of weapons, and where are the key factories? Is the war effort fully supported by the people or are there discontented groups that could be encouraged to resist it? The means of espionage include not just the work of spies but such other business as photographs and sightings made from flights of aircraft over enemy territory; intercepted radio messages; gleanings from enemy newspapers, books, maps and government publications; reports from neutral diplomats in enemy countries; and interrogation of prisoners of war.

Counterespionage is partly an effort to protect your own secrets from the thrusts of enemy espionage. Even more important, perhaps, is the effort to find out who the enemy's spies are and what other methods of espionage he is trying. Then you work to neutralize or thwart the activity in some way. If you have caught a spy, you can hope to turn him into a double agent. If he seems to be too dangerous or unreliable for that, you might execute him or imprison him. A valuable by-product of counterespionage is the picture it yields of what the enemy wants to know.

Deception is really a form of counterespionage, but it is so special that it deserves separate mention. The aim is to give the enemy's espionage apparatus the wrong ideas. General Sir Archibald Wavell, one of England's heroes in World War II, wrote that the "elementary principle of all deception is to attract the enemy's attention to what you wish him to see and to distract his attention from what you do not wish him to see." The Allies carried out some spectacular deceptions during World War II, including Project Fortitude, concerned with the invasion of France, and Operation Mincemeat, concerned with the invasion of Sicily.

Taken altogether, the espionage, counterespionage and deception operations in World War II added up to a big business. One measure of the extent of the operations is provided by Captain W. J. Holmes, who served as a U.S. naval intelligence officer in the Pacific theater. He wrote that in the period between the end of the war in Europe in May 1945 and the end of the war in the Pacific three months later, a single intelligence operation—the U.S. Navy's Joint Intelligence Center, Pacific Ocean Area (JICPOA)—had a staff of 1,800 people in Hawaii and hundreds of others elsewhere, and put out each week an average of two million sheets of printed information and more than 150,000 photographs.

Another measure comes from William J. Casey, who served in the London office of the U.S. Office of Strategic Services (OSS) during the war and later became head of the Central Intelligence Agency. He reported on the output of just one source, BCRA, which was the intelligence service of the French exile regime in London. Its information on conditions in German-occupied France was important in 1944. "By 1944," Casey wrote, "BCRA was distributing reports to the entire London intelligence community twice a day. The monthly output of this information factory averaged 200,000 mimeographed sheets, 60,000 copies of maps and sketches and 10,000 photographic reproductions."

This, then, was the secret war. It was played out behind the scenes of the public war—the great battles and strategic moves that were reported in the newspapers and on the radio.

The public war had its roots in the peace settlement that ended World War I (1914–1918) and in the widespread hardships of the economic depression of the 1930s. Many Germans thought the terms of the Treaty of Versailles, which formally ended World War I, were humiliating and harsh for their country. With their support the National Socialist (Nazi) party, led by Adolf Hitler, came to power in 1933, promising to restore order in the economy and to renew Germany's glory by expanding its boundaries. Hitler soon won dictatorial power and began preparing the nation for a war of conquest.

By 1938, he was ready to strike. Germany took over Austria in March 1938 and Czechoslovakia in March 1939. Two months later Hitler formed a military alliance with Italy, which was under the dictatorship of Benito Mussolini. On September 1, 1939, Hitler's forces invaded Poland, provoking England and France to declare war on Germany two days later in a belated effort to halt Hitler's aggression.

The declaration of war did little to slow the German juggernaut. In 1940 German forces overran Denmark, Norway, the Netherlands and Belgium. That spring they outflanked the Maginot Line that the French had built for defense and swept into France. By June the French had crumbled and England stood alone. Winston Churchill, newly installed as Britain's prime minister, put the situation eloquently in a speech to the House of Commons:

The Battle of France is over. I expect that the Battle of Britain is about to begin . . . .The whole fury and might of the enemy must very soon be turned on us. Hitler knows that he will have to break us in this Island or lose the war. If we can stand up to him, all Europe may be free and the life of the world may move forward into broad, sunlit uplands. But if we fail, then the whole world, including the United States, including all that we have known and cared for, will sink into the abyss of a new Dark Age . . . Let us therefore brace ourselves to our duties, and so bear ourselves that, if the British Empire and its Commonwealth last for a thousand years, men will still say, "This was their finest hour."

Hitler did indeed turn his whole fury and might on England. Under the code name of Operation Sealion he planned an invasion of the British Isles. As a prelude he mounted heavy

The British cabinet met in this underground room near the prime minister's official residence in London when the city was under attack from German bombers or V bombs. Prime Minister Winston Churchill occupied the round-backed chair near the world map at the left. This room and several other rooms in the complex called the Cabinet War Rooms remain as they were during the war and are open as a museum. (Imperial War Museum)

bombing attacks on England, starting in August 1940. The aim was to weaken British defenses so that the invasion would be easy and perhaps even unnecessary if the British should be so demoralized as to surrender.

A British Spitfire fighter attacks a German Dornier bomber at the height of the Battle of Britain in 1940. The British, heavily outmanned, were aided in directing their fighters to the right places by Ultra, which had broken the German codes. (National Archives)

The British were far from demoralized. Between August and October 1940, the Royal Air Force—overmatched and outgunned by the German Luftwaffe but helped by Ultra to know when and where the attacks would come—fought off the German effort in *what has become known as the Battle of Britain.* ("*Never in the field of human conflict was so much owed by so many to so few,*" Churchill said of the RAF's achievement.) With winter coming, Hitler postponed Sealion. He was never able to return to the plan, because in June of 1941 he made what turned out to be his worst strategic mistake by invading Russia, thus creating for his forces a two-front war and making Russia an ally of the West.

The mistake was not apparent immediately because the Germans at first advanced easily into Russia. And in other areas Hitler's forces continued to score victories. German submarines wreaked devastation on Allied shipping in the Atlantic, and German troops gained ground in North Africa.

Meanwhile, a militaristic regime in Japan had been thrusting outward in a move to create a "Greater East Asia Co-Prosperity Sphere" with Japan as the dominant power. Japan went to war with China in 1931 and steadily built up strength for further adventures. The adventure that turned out to be Japan's worst strategic mistake came 10 years after the move into China. On December 7, 1941, the Japanese launched their devastating surprise attack on the American base at Pearl Harbor in Hawaii, thereby bringing the United States into the war. Again, however, the mistake was not immediately apparent because Japan progressed through a series of victories. In short order Japanese forces conquered the Philippines, Malaya, Burma, Indonesia and many islands in the Pacific.

With Germany ascendant in Europe and North Africa and Japan bestriding the Pacific, things looked dark for the Allies in the summer of 1942. But gradually, aided especially by the ability of American industry to turn out planes, ships and weapons in quantity, the tide began to turn. The U.S. Navy scored its first successes against the Japanese fleet, notably at the battle of the Coral Sea in May 1942 and the battle of Midway in June. The Allies invaded North Africa in the fall of 1942, and by the following spring they had cleared the Germans out of Africa. The Russians steadily pushed Hitler's forces back toward Germany. In the Atlantic the American and British naval forces began to take a heavy toll of German submarines, gradually breaking the back of Hitler's offensive against Allied shipping. In 1943 the Allies invaded Italy, which surrendered in September, leaving only the Germans to counter the northward advance of Allied troops. By 1944 Allied bombers were pounding Germany so severely that Hitler's cities, industry and communications were in disarray. In June 1944 the Allies made their major move—an invasion of Europe launched from England against the French coast. Soon they too were pushing Hitler's forces back toward Germany. Crushed by the eastward movement of the Americans and British, the westward movement of the Russians and the relentless bombing, Germany surrendered in May 1945.

In the Pacific, the Allies were moving steadily from island to island toward Japan. The Japanese navy was in tatters, and few supplies were reaching Japan because of the stranglehold applied to Japanese merchant shipping by American submarines. In August 1945, shattered by American atomic bombs dropped on Hiroshima and Nagasaki, the Japanese surrendered. The war was over.

During all these years, the participants in the secret war made their important but largely invisible contribution to the outcome. The contribution can be summed up in one word: foreknowledge. If you know what the enemy will do, or is capable of doing, you are better prepared to deal with him than if he takes you by surprise. Due to the nature of the business, it was only years later that the names of some of the participants in the secret war became known and some of their achievements were revealed. The pages that follow will tell the story of the secret part of World War II more fully, describing first the major players and then the activities of the Japanese, the Germans, the British and the Americans. Finally, the book will set forth some of the remarkable achievements of Ultra and its American counterpart, known appropriately as Magic.

1

THE PLAYERS
The Stage Is Set for the Secret War

The one to watch, above all the thousands of others who worked in espionage or counterespionage in World War II, is Canaris. Admiral Wilhelm Canaris had had a successful career in the German navy when he was named head of the Abwehr, a branch of the army that was the main German intelligence service, in 1935. He remained in that post until almost the end of the war. The question to keep in mind is how well he served his Nazi masters. There is evidence that he, like many other prominent Germans, saw the dictator Adolf Hitler and his Nazi party as bad for Germany and therefore may have leaned toward helping the Allies when he thought he could. If so, it seems fair to say that he believed he was acting in the long-term interest of his country.

Although Canaris was only 47 years old when he took charge of the Abwehr, his hair was already white. Hence people in the organization referred to him (probably not in his presence) as "Old Whitehead." One of his biographers, the German writer Karl Heinz Abshagen, has described him as "a man careful in all things, one who weighed every possibility, examined every move, alternately pushed forward and held back by his intuitions, always hiding his real thoughts and plans."

The organization Canaris headed operated out of two former townhouses at 76/78 Tirpitzufer in Berlin. Canaris's office was on the top floor, reached by an ancient elevator that sometimes refused to function. "The room," Abshagen wrote, "was most unpretentious. Canaris never appeared to consider that the arrangements and the furnishings of his own office were hardly suitable for a man of his position." The arrangements included an ancient Persian carpet, an ink-stained desk bearing a model of the German cruiser *Dresden* and a cot loaded with blankets, atop which Canaris's beloved dachshund, Seppl, could often be found snoozing.

Admiral Wilhelm Canaris (right) talks with two German soldiers. Canaris was head of the Abwehr, the German intelligence service, during most of the war. (National Archives)

Canaris presided over an organization with three main arms. Abwehr I was the espionage arm, collecting information from German and foreign spies who operated in the major cities of Europe, the Near East and the United States. Abwehr II managed German efforts to sabotage its enemies. Abwehr III did counterespionage inside Germany.

Another German espionage organization, often at odds with Canaris and the Abwehr, was the Sicherheitsdienst, usually known as the SD. It was the Nazi Party's intelligence arm, which ruthlessly sought out enemies of the regime in Germany and in countries conquered by Germany. Its head from 1931 until midway into World War II was Reinhard Heydrich, who will appear in this story again in a particularly dramatic episode that cost him his life. Another prominent member of the SD was Walter Schellenberg, who will also appear later in this story in connection with the remarkable Venlo incident. He became the working head of the SD when it absorbed the Abwehr in 1944.

Schellenberg published his memoirs after the war. His description of his office at the time when he was head of the foreign department of the SD reveals something of the kind of man he was.

> Microphones were hidden everywhere, in the walls, under the desk, even in one of the lamps, so that every conversation and every sound was automatically recorded . . .
>
> My desk was like a small fortress. Two automatic guns were built into it which could spray the whole room with bullets. These guns pointed at the visitor and followed his or her progress towards my desk. All I had to do in an emergency was to press a button and both guns would fire simultaneously. At the same time I could press another button and a siren would summon the guards to surround the building and block every exit.

✳✳✳

Japan faced one main enemy, the United States, in a war waged throughout the Pacific Ocean. Hence its leading espionage organization was naval—the Third Bureau of the Naval General Staff. Section 5 of the bureau was specifically concerned with spying on the United States. Before the war, the section had a number of spies in this country, chiefly on the West Coast. After the war started, that network withered. For one thing, the United States rounded up most of the Japanese people who were here when the war started and put them in internment camps. Another problem for the

Third Bureau was that any Japanese person was highly conspicuous in a country with few Oriental residents, so that it became virtually impossible for the bureau to set up and maintain a functioning spy after the war began.

Things were easier in Hawaii, which became a focus of Japanese interest a few years before the war when Admiral Isoroku Yamamoto, commander-in-chief of Japan's Combined Imperial Fleet, conceived the plan of destroying the American Pacific Fleet based at Pearl Harbor. He called on Captain Kanji Ogawa, chief of the Third Bureau's Section 5, to build up a file of information on the fleet and on conditions in Hawaii.

Ogawa was diligent. He set up a network of spies in Hawaii. One of them was a German, Bernard Kuehn; Ogawa had met him on a beach in Japan. Another was the proprietor of the Venice Cafe, who was able to overhear the conversations of the American sailors who frequented the place. Ogawa also sent to Hawaii a young man who had been a naval intelligence officer specializing in American affairs until illness forced him out of the navy. This was former Ensign Takeo Yoshikawa, but in Hawaii he went under the name of Tadashi Morimura and the title of assistant to the vice consul. "Morimura" was scarcely noticed as he bustled about the islands collecting information on the American fleet.

Ogawa had other sources of information about the fleet. His people listened in on the fleet's radio traffic and thereby learned much about what ships were active, where they were and what kind of maneuvers they carried out. Japanese submarines lurking in the waters of Hawaii kept an eye on American ships. The representatives of Japanese firms doing business in Hawaii contributed information too.

Japan also made good use of her diplomats in Washington (until they were ejected at the start of the war) and in other capitals. One diplomat who actually turned out to be a mine of information for the Allies, although that was certainly not his intention, was the Japanese ambassador in Berlin, General Hiroshi Baron Oshima. Germany and Japan agreed to exchange information once they were both in the war against the United States, and so Oshima sent long reports to Tokyo about German strategy and actions. Thanks to Ultra, his reports were in Allied hands as soon as he sent them.

***

The British were old hands at the spy trade, with a secret intelligence service that had been established in the time of Queen Elizabeth I. By World War II the organization was known variously as MI-6 (the letters standing for military intelligence), SIS (Secret Intelligence Service), and Broadway (from its address at 54 Broadway in London, which to passersby was identified at first as being the place of business of the Minimax Fire Extinguisher Company and later as being occupied by the Government Communications Department). Throughout the war its chief was Stewart Graham Menzies, a member of a wealthy Scottish family that had close ties to the royal family. (Indeed, there were rumors that Menzies was the illegitimate son of the Prince of Wales, who in 1901 became King Edward VII.) The pronunciation of Menzies's surname, as is so often the case with proper names in England, bore little relation to the spelling: It was "Mingiss." To the people in SIS he was known, as all its recent chiefs have been, as "C," a designation deriving from the name of Captain Sir Mansfield Cumming, who headed SIS from 1909 to 1923.

To many people who did not know him well, Menzies appeared to be interested mainly in his social clubs, his fox hunting, his card playing and other diversions of the British aristocracy. He was, in fact, keenly intelligent and highly determined. Kim Philby, who served prominently in MI-6 during the war and was only later revealed as a Soviet agent, gives a picture of Menzies in *My Silent War*:

> Broadway was a dingy building, a warren of wooden partitions and frosted glass windows. It had eight floors served by an ancient lift [elevator]. On one of my early visits, I got into the lift with a colleague whom the liftman treated with obtrusive deference. The

stranger gave me a swift glance and looked away. He was well-built and well-dressed, but what struck me most was his pallor: pale face, pale eyes, silvery blond hair thinning on top—the whole an impression of pepper-and-salt. When he got out at the fourth floor, I asked the liftman who he was. 'Why, sir, that's the Chief,' he answered in some surprise.

As "C," Menzies was one of the few officials to carry "The Ivory," an ivory plaque signifying that the bearer was a trusted and important servant of the crown who might need to be with the king in a time of crisis. Menzies had the right of access to the king, the prime minister and the foreign secretary at any hour. He came to be a friend and confidant of the wartime prime minister, Winston Churchill, and met with him alone regularly—often at the late night or early morning hours favored by that extraordinary man.

Several other British players will appear on this stage. MI-5 was the internal security organization, in charge of hunting down spies who were at work in the United Kingdom. It was the counterpart of the Federal Bureau of Investigation (FBI) in the United States. MI-5 said after the war that it had rounded up every spy the Germans tried to establish in the United Kingdom.

SOE (the Special Operations Executive), created by Churchill in 1940 with instructions from him to "set Europe ablaze," had the role of helping resistance groups in territory occupied by the Germans and organizing sabotage against German operations. Its head from 1943 until the end of the war was Major General Sir Colin McVean Gubbins. Talking in 1948 of what SOE had sought to do, he said:

> The shock of initial German success was profound, particularly in the occupied territories of Western Europe. France, Belgium, Holland, Denmark and Norway lay as if stunned; only the Poles, toughened by centuries of oppression, were spiritually uncrushed. Yet in all these countries there were hundreds of thousands of individuals who refused to accept defeat and who prayed for the means to continue the struggle.
>
> The British Commonwealth was on the defensive and it was clear that it would be years before invasion would be possible; what

could, however, be done in the meantime was to attack the enemy by unorthodox methods: attack his war potential wherever it was exposed and at least create some running sores to drain his strength and to disperse his forces. This would give the maximum of assistance to the forces of liberation when the invasion of the Continent finally did take place. To undertake this task, an organization, Special Operations Executive, was created.

This late-Victorian mansion at Bletchley Park served as headquarters of the Government Code and Cypher School, the group that broke the German codes and read them throughout the war. The low white building at the right is one of the many "huts" built on the ground to accommodate the growing staff. (U.S. Army Intelligence and Security Command)

Then there was GC&CS, the Government Code and Cypher School, also known irreverently to people who worked there as the Golf, Cheese and Chess Society. It is better known as Bletchley, a name deriving from its headquarters in the mansion and in temporary buildings on the grounds of Bletchley Park, a late-Victorian country estate some 40 miles north of London. One should not be irreverent about Bletchley, however, because it was the center of the code-breaking operation—the place where Ultra became a reality.

And there was LCS, the London Controlling Section, created by Churchill in 1941 to oversee the "special means" of Britain's secret war. "Special means" encompassed the massive program intended to deceive the Germans. Wavell, who had a hand in the formation of LCS, said that its aim should be "to force the enemy to DO SOMETHING that will assist our operations, e.g., to move his reserves to the wrong place or to refrain from moving to the right place . . . or to induce the enemy to waste his effort." The head of LCS was Colonel John Henry Bevan. General John R. Deane of the U.S. Army said of him, "Colonel Bevan played his games with great skill and never let his right hand know what his left hand was up to."

And there was the XX Committee, also known as the Twenty Committee and the Double-Cross Committee because the Roman numeral XX represents 20 and can also be read as a double cross. The committee had the crucial and difficult job of controlling the German spies who had been turned into double agents. Through them it played a major part in the deception program. A key figure on the XX Committee was John C. Masterman of the University of Oxford, a scholar and teacher who also wrote mystery stories. In his view, the task of the committee was to put German spies out of business or to persuade them to work for the British. As he wrote later, "If the Germans are receiving an adequate service of news from our controlled agents, they will not expend a great deal of time and effort to establish another system as well."

Finally, there was William S. Stephenson, a wealthy Canadian industrialist and inventor who served in New York as head of British Security Coordination. Under the code name of Intrepid, he and his organization helped the unpracticed American intelligence agencies track down German spies in the Western Hemisphere, intercept coded messages and penetrate hostile diplomatic missions in North and South America.

***

The Americans, unlike the British, had no long tradition of intelligence work and no central intelligence agency. As the writer John Chamberlain put it, referring to places the United States might need information about to conduct the war:

> If you wanted a Michelin road map of the Vosges or Haute Savoie in the Washington of early 1941, it was a hundred to one that you could not find one. Nor could you successfully apply to any governmental agency for the gauge of an Algerian railroad track, the kilowatt-hour supply of the Japanese power grid, the number of wharfside cranes in Casablanca, the quality of drinking water in Tunis, the tilt of the beaches of Kyushu or the texture of the Iwo Jima soil.

The first move by President Franklin D. Roosevelt to fill this need was to create, in 1941, the Office of the Coordinator of Information. As its head he named William J. Donovan, a prominent New York lawyer who had run as the Republican nominee for governor in 1932. (That was the year Roosevelt, then governor of New York, was elected president for the first of four terms. He lived less than three months into his fourth term, dying suddenly of a stroke on April 12, 1945, and so not seeing the successful outcome of the war effort he had led.) In 1942, recognizing that espionage and information activities did not fit well together, Roosevelt separated them, creating the Office of Strategic Services as the central intelligence office and making Donovan its chief. "You will have to begin with nothing," the president told Donovan.

Donovan was a man who could begin with nothing and in short order create a considerable something. At the time of his appointment, he was well known in the country as "Wild Bill" Donovan for his exploits as commander of the first battalion of the 69th Infantry Regiment and battlefield commander of the regiment in World War I—exploits that won him the Congressional Medal of Honor. Prodigiously energetic and a fountainhead of ideas, he soon had OSS organized into three main arms. "R&A," the research and analysis arm, rounded up the kind of information Chamberlain described. "MO," the morale operations arm, took charge of propaganda and deception against the enemy. "SI," the secret intelligence arm, carried out the spying and the sabotage. By the end of the war, OSS had grown to an organization with a staff of some 12,000 people and an annual budget of about $57 million.

William J. Donovan served as head of the U.S. Office of Strategic Services (OSS) throughout the war. The OSS was the nation's first centralized intelligence agency. (National Archives)

The OSS was not the only American intelligence agency during the war. Also on the scene, as they had been for many years, were MI (Military Intelligence, the army's intelligence arm, headed by General George V. Strong) and ONI (the Office of Naval Intelligence, which had a succession of directors). Those organizations viewed the arrival of OSS with little enthusiasm. In its early days, they had access to Ultra and Magic and the OSS did not—a situation that put OSS at a disadvantage. After Donovan complained, Roosevelt ordered MI and ONI to make some Ultra and Magic information available to OSS, but he left them the power to decide what information it should be. The handicap affected OSS throughout the war.

A month after the war ended, President Harry S Truman dissolved the OSS. (Truman's middle initial stood for nothing, and he preferred it to be printed without a period.) The OSS had established the tradition of a central intelligence organization, however, and Truman said as he signed the order ending it that he intended to continue the tradition in a somewhat different way. Two years later, Congress passed and Truman signed the National Security Act, creating the CIA (Central Intelligence Agency) to carry on the tradition.

2

JAPAN MOVES
Years of Preparation for Pearl Harbor

The Japanese had an advantage. Influential men in the government turned their thoughts to the possibility of war with the United States long before they actually launched the war by attacking Pearl Harbor on December 7, 1941. And so, throughout the 1930s, their preparations for war included the establishment of spy networks not only in the United States but also in Mexico and Central America, the Pacific, Asia and Europe.

Their main entry to the United States was by means of young naval officers sent to this country as "language students." Dozens of them came every year, and their first stop was Washington. There they checked in with Taro Terasaki, whose title was second secretary at the Japanese embassy but whose real function was as mastermind of his country's espionage network in the Western Hemisphere. Terasaki told each of them what to do, which usually was to enroll at a university or technical school near West Coast seaports. There the student could report on ship traffic, naval training, the construction of warships and activity in the port, such as what kinds of goods were moving in and out.

But Terasaki was working on more than that. His agents cultivated people who might oppose an American war effort. Among them were members of the America First group, and also influential black leaders. The Japanese hoped the work with the blacks would lead to racial troubles that, as one of their messages to Tokyo put it, would "stall the program of U.S. plans for national defense." Terasaki's people also maintained ties with Nisei—Japanese-Americans—working in American defense plants and serving in the army and navy.

Another operation was run by the office of the naval attaché in the Japanese embassy. FBI documents made public after the war revealed that the attaché's branch office in New York was spending $500,000 a month on intelligence activity. That is a lot of money now; it was a huge amount then. Most of it went for technical information and for buying such things as aircraft parts and radios in order to get a good look at them. On the West Coast the branches of Japanese corporations provided cover for naval spies and helped them communicate with Tokyo.

One of the naval spies was Lieutenant Commander Togami, who worked as an undercover agent. With an assistant he set out in 1937 to make an automobile tour of the United States. They had a shortwave radio receiver hidden in the trunk of the car. Going from one naval base to another and living in rented quarters near each one, they used the receiver to listen in on radio signals between ship and shore. The exercise yielded to the Japanese navy an abundance of information about American naval equipment and tactics.

One of their useful findings was that the U.S. Navy was less skilled than the Japanese navy in night fighting. In the early months of the war Japanese ships regularly attacked American ships at night and usually came off better. The Japanese also concluded from the data turned in by Togami that the U.S. Navy was at its highest level of training and efficiency in June, whereas the Japanese navy peaked in December. The Japanese navy attacked Pearl Harbor in December.

A look at a map will show why the Japanese found it worthwhile to set up a network of agents south of the

American border. The Gulf of California extends 800 miles into western Mexico, reaching almost to California. In a war the Japanese would have a hard time attacking the United States directly from the Pacific Ocean, but naval bases along the gulf and land bases in Baja California (the part of Mexico west of the gulf) would give them a strategic foothold. Japan cultivated Mexico's good will and kept track of the situation in the entire region by establishing spies in Mexico and throughout Central America to the Panama Canal. Thus it was that Japanese "fishing fleets" were busy in the gulf and in the ocean nearby. Many of the crew members were in fact naval officers posing as ordinary seamen. The task of the "fishermen" was to keep track of American naval operations off the California coast.

On land, and particularly in the Panama Canal Zone, many Japanese spies posed as dentists, barbers and storekeepers. Serving the hundreds of American sailors and soldiers in the Canal Zone, they had only to listen to pick up information about the military situation in that vital corridor between the Atlantic and the Pacific.

It was also plain to the Japanese that a war in the Pacific would involve action against the British, who had colonies throughout the Far East. In every colony, therefore, the Japanese set up before the war a team of espionage agents headed by a naval-intelligence officer in disguise. With those teams Tokyo kept in touch with the strengths and weaknesses of the British colonies. Partly as a result of this effort, the colonies fell to the Japanese quickly when the war started.

The Japanese task was made easier by a deal that the Third Bureau and the Abwehr worked out in 1935. One part of the agreement was that Japan would focus its espionage work on Asia and the Soviet Union, and Germany would focus on Europe and the Western Hemisphere. That meant the Japanese would have Germans and other people who did not look Japanese spying for them in the United States and Great Britain.

The other part of the deal was that the two sides would exchange information. That helped to supply the bulk of the reports that Ambassador Oshima in Berlin sent to Tokyo. It also gave Japan access to such fancy German espionage devices as *Mikropunkt* and *Aku-Gerat*. *Mikropunkt*, or microdot, was a means of compressing a written message into a dot the size of a period at the end of a sentence. The dots could then be pasted onto an ordinary letter or report over the letters *i* and *j* and at the end of sentences. If you knew they might be there, you could find them by holding the paper up to a light, but that was slow and difficult work. *Aku-Gerat* was a small radio containing both a transmitter and a receiver. It was so compact that it could be hidden in the false bottom of a suitcase.

Much of espionage depends on slyness and on trick devices like microdot and hidden radios, but sometimes the spymasters take less subtle approaches. In 1937, the Japanese simply broke into the American consulate in Kobe and cracked the safe. (They had done some subtle spying beforehand and knew what was in the safe and the time of night when conditions were right for an undetected break-in.) With the safe open, they pulled out the American "Brown" code and the M-138 enciphering device and took photographs of them. The information was soon put to good use when the Japanese built their first radio-interception station at Owada, a village near Tokyo. There, and later at other places, they listened in knowledgeably on the coded radio traffic of American naval vessels and picked up a great deal of information about the fleet and the nature of its maneuvers.

Access to codes, however, was not enough. The grand aim of the Japanese in their plans for war was to establish what they called the Greater East Asia Co-Prosperity Sphere. What that really meant was that they would control much of the Pacific territory to their south and would have access to its food and raw materials, both of which Japan needed to carry on its war with China (which started in 1931) and to carry on its planned aggression against American and British territory in the Pacific.

In pursuit of this aim, Japan needed firsthand and day-to-day information about such matters as the number of planes the RAF (Britain's Royal Air Force) had at its bases in the Pacific area; troop strength and movement; and naval

Admiral Isoroku Yamamoto was the architect of the Japanese attack on Pearl Harbor. American fighter planes, alerted by the code-breaking operation called Magic, later shot him down over the Pacific. (U.S. Army Intelligence and Security Command)

strength and activity, together with the need to know what the American navy was up to at Pearl Harbor and elsewhere in the Pacific. Typical of the way they went about getting the information was their establishment of Unit 82 in Taiwan. Its head was Colonel Yoshiide Hayashi. He quickly set up a network of agents in Thailand, Malaya and Burma. Hayashi also enlisted ship captains to report on what they saw in their travels through the area. At a time when aerial reconnaissance was in its infancy, Unit 82 had an airplane and crew that concentrated on photographing airfields, harbors, roads and military installations. The information turned up by Unit 82 and other sources showed the Japanese that their potential enemies in the South Pacific were weak and unprepared for war.

Then there was the operation at Pearl Harbor. OpZ was the name Yamamoto gave his plan to attack the harbor. The aim was to destroy or at least severely damage the American Pacific Fleet, which was based there, before it could get out into the Pacific and start interfering with Japan's move toward the territories in the South Pacific that it planned to absorb in the Greater East Asia Co-Prosperity Sphere. OpZ required Ogawa and Section 5 of the Third Bureau to switch their primary focus from the American mainland to Pearl Harbor.

Enter former ensign Yoshikawa, who arrived in Honolulu four months before the attack on Pearl Harbor. In his guise as vice-consul Morimura, posing as a heavy drinker and party lover, he did not seem to be spy material. Indeed, American counterintelligence took so little notice of him that they left him off all their lists of people they thought might be spying for the Japanese. (The suspects were graded A, B or C, according to how dangerous they were thought to be.)

So, unsuspected, Yoshikawa set about learning the conditions at Pearl Harbor. He went swimming to find out about beach gradients and underwater obstructions. He went out in boats to see what protective nets were in the water. He took bicycle rides to watch the American patrol planes, so that he could learn their schedule and range. And he hung around in bars listening to the sailors.

Finally, Yoshikawa drew a map of Pearl Harbor, showing exactly where the navy ships were berthed. And, on a map of the island of Oahu, he marked the location of the airfields.

Early in November, the Japanese merchant ship *Taiyo Maru* tied up at a dock in Honolulu. One of her crew, listed as a steward, was in fact Lieutenant Commander Suguro Suzuki of the Japanese navy. Suzuki went ashore and made his way to the Japanese consulate. There he gave the consul, Nagao Kita, a piece of rice paper that he had crumpled into a small ball. On it were nearly 100 questions about the Pearl Harbor defenses. One of them was: On what day of the week

This aerial view of the large American naval base at Pearl Harbor in Hawaii was made a few weeks before the Japanese attack on December 7, 1941. Japanese spies had bought postcards carrying a similar view, and the attacking Japanese bomber pilots used the postcard view as a guide. (National Archives)

would the largest number of ships be in the harbor? Kita passed the list on to the industrious Yoshikawa.

Suzuki then went out to do some shopping in Honolulu. Among the things he bought were several sets of postcards showing views of Pearl Harbor from the air. The price was $1 per set. Eventually Suzuki went back to his ship. And eventually Yoshikawa arrived at the dock, went aboard the ship and closeted himself with Suzuki. During the meeting,= Yoshikawa turned over his maps and sketches and the answers to the questions about Pearl Harbor. The answer to the question about the day of the week when the most ships would be in the harbor: Sunday.

The attack came on a Sunday, less than five weeks later. In the cockpits of the attacking planes were copies of the postcard pictures of the harbor. The one change in them was that the scene had been marked off into numbered squares. Each pilot had a particular square to attack. Thanks to the work of Yoshikawa, all the pilots knew exactly which ships would be there.

Yoshikawa was not the only one to spy on Pearl Harbor before the attack. There was also Kuehn, the German, who moved to Honolulu in 1936 with his wife Friedel and daughter Ruth. Friedel and Ruth opened a beauty parlor near Honolulu. Many of their customers were wives of American naval people. The wives tended to talk a lot about the comings and goings of their husbands, thereby giving Friedel and Ruth news about the comings and goings of American naval vessels.

Kuehn, meanwhile, kept his eyes and ears open, reporting what he saw and heard to the Japanese consulate and sometimes to the Third Bureau in Tokyo by radio. By late 1941, it was apparent to him that a day might come when it would be difficult for him to communicate with his Japanese masters. He therefore proposed an elaborate code. A light in a dormer window of his house would, depending on the time of day, tell what types of ships were at Pearl Harbor. Another code involved numbers on the sail of his sailboat. He was also prepared to put phony personal messages on radio station KGMB in Honolulu; certain phrases would convey secret messages to the radio operators on Japanese ships.

Kuehn and his family were on the "A" list of American counterintelligence, and they were arrested shortly after the

President Franklin D. Roosevelt signs the U.S. declaration of war against Japan on December 8, 1941, the day after the Japanese attack on Pearl Harbor. The president wears a black band in honor of the Americans killed in the attack. (National Archives)

attack on Pearl Harbor. The Japanese had not forewarned him of the attack, and he did not get to use his code scheme. Yoshikawa, when counterintelligence finally caught on to his activity, was arrested and then returned to Japan.

An irony about the work of Yoshikawa is that American law helped him. Japanese ships at sea sent by radio a daily message on the weather—an important bit of intelligence in the days before weather satellites, when ships were the only source of meteorological information over vast areas of the Pacific. The first two cipher groups of the daily message gave the ship's location.

American intelligence, seeking to keep track of the positions of Japanese ships, went to the commercial radio company in Honolulu that handled the messages and asked about picking up a list of ship locations every day. The answer was no: The Federal Communications Act prohibited the disclosure of a message to anyone but the addressee.

This was at the time when Yoshikawa was sending his coded messages to Tokyo through the same radio company in Honolulu. Those messages also came under the protection of the Federal Communications Act.

The story has a further twist, related by W. J. Holmes, who was an American naval-intelligence officer in Honolulu.

In the summer of 1941, information on the location of naval ships was classified (made secret). Only the captain of the yard (and Yoshikawa) had up-to-date information on every ship's berthing assignment at the many docks and anchorages of Pearl Harbor. Sometimes a navy officer looking for his ship would be told that the information was classified. He could go to the heights above Pearl Harbor and pick out his ship. Often such an officer might encounter Yoshikawa, who regularly made such observations and promptly reported them to Tokyo.

***

One day Mary Wallace of Springfield, Ohio, stopped in at a doll shop on Madison Avenue in New York and bought three dolls. On June 22, 1942, she received at her home in Springfield a letter marked "Return to sender." No doubt about it: the return address read "Mrs. Mary Wallace, 1808 East High St., Springfield, Ohio." But Mrs. Wallace had not written the letter, which had been addressed to Señora Inez Lopez de Molinali in Buenos Aires.

The letter, signed "Mary Wallace," read in part: "The only new dolls I have are THREE LOVELY IRISH DOLLS . . . You wrote me that you had sent a letter to Mr. Shaw, well I went to see Mr. Shaw and he destroyed your letter . . . His car damaged but is being repaired now."

Mrs. Wallace was mystified. She was also suspicious, because the odd wording suggested that some message other than the written one was being conveyed. She took the letter to the postal authorities, and they turned it over to the FBI.

At about the same time, another letter, marked "unknown at this address," was returned to a woman in Portland, Oregon, from Buenos Aires. She had not written the letter, which spoke of a damaged Siamese doll. Soon the FBI had laid hands on several similar letters having to do with dolls. Cryptanalysts went to work on the letters and decided that the dolls represented a code for naval intelligence. The three Irish dolls, for example, stood for "three new American warships," and a reference to "a doll in a hula skirt" meant a ship just in from Hawaii.

Who had sent the letters? It took the FBI a while to find out, but eventually the trail led to the doll shop on Madison Avenue. The proprietor, Velvalee Dickinson, was an unlikely spy, but a spy she was. Before the war, she and her husband had become friendly with Japanese diplomats in San Francisco. They continued their interest in Japan after they moved to New York, and eventually they agreed to become spies. Mrs. Dickinson carried on after her husband died. The doll shop was a cover for her activity. Her messages were addressed to a Japanese agent in Buenos Aires. What undid her was an uncharacteristic bit of carelessness on the part of the Japanese. They replaced the agent in Buenos Aires and gave up the address, neglecting to tell Mrs. Dickinson. Soon her letters, bearing as return addresses the names of women who had been customers of the doll shop, began coming back to the United States, marked "Return to sender." The return addresses had been a means of cover for Mrs. Dickinson; in the end they became the means of uncovering her activity. The activity ended when she was arrested and sentenced to 10 years in prison.

3

GERMANY MOVES
Canaris Against (Or Was He?) the Allies

The scene is Canaris's office, the date September 21, 1939—the 20th anniversary of the Abwehr's founding. Canaris is reading a report from "Johnny," Abwehr agent A.3504. Johnny has been a German spy in England for several years, and the Germans regard him highly. His report says: "Installation of net of UHF [ultra-high-frequency] stations to monitor approaching enemy aircraft all along coast from Isle of Wight to Orkneys." This is hot news for the Germans, who are concerned that the British may be setting up radar defenses but are not sure the antennas they have photographed along the British coast are for radar. "You know, gentlemen," Canaris says to the aides who have brought him the report, "this may yet turn out to be one of the most important pieces of intelligence we'll ever get in this rat race. It's the nicest [Abwehr] birthday present I dared to expect."

What Canaris and the Abwehr do not know is that Johnny and his radio are in Wandsworth Prison in London and that Johnny is operating as SNOW, one of the first German spies turned by the British into a double agent. It is important to the British to lead the Germans on by having the double agents send them information that is believable and seems to be useful. In the case of the radar, the Germans were onto the information already and certainly would have found out when the radar began operating and their planes began to penetrate the network.

This double agent was in fact Alfred George Owens, a Canadian electrical engineer with good contacts in Germany. He had volunteered his service to MI-6 in 1936 and thereafter was recruited by the Abwehr. As Masterman wrote in his report on the work of the XX Committee: "Substantially from the end of 1936 until the outbreak of war, SNOW worked as a straightforward German agent, whose activities, although known to the authorities, were not interfered with in any important respect." With the beginning of the war in 1939, however, the British reined him in, and "with SNOW's first message from Wandsworth

This early British radar installation and others like it were of great interest to German spies because the Abwehr foresaw that radar would help British defenses against German bomber attacks in what became known as the Battle of Britain. (National Archives)

Prison the double-cross system was well and truly launched."

The Owens story is in many ways the story of German espionage in World War II. The Germans put a lot of effort into spying and had a big organization for it, but the results were thin and often harmful to German interests. Let us follow the trail.

For several years before the war, the Abwehr organized and ran a fair number of spy rings in the United States. The head of one of them was Nikolaus Ritter, to whom Canaris had given the task of finding out about the Norden bombsight. The bombsight was one of America's most closely guarded military secrets, because it enabled bomber planes to find their targets with great accuracy. In 1937, Ritter made contact with Hermann Lang, who had come to the United States from Germany and had become an American citizen. Lang had a pivotal job in the Norden factory. As part of the effort to keep the bombsight secret, the Norden company had different teams assemble different parts of it. Each team worked from a set of blueprints covering that team's part of the project. Lang's job was to hand out the blueprints and to collect them again when the team had finished with them. When he had a set that he could keep overnight, he took them home and copied the drawings on tracing paper.

Set by set, he passed the copies to Ritter, who sent them on to Germany. (One drawing was so large that Ritter had to get Abwehr agent F.2341, a steward on the German passenger ship *Bremen*, to smuggle it onto the ship in a rolled-up umbrella.) Lang could not provide all the details about the bombsight. By the time the Luftwaffe (the German air force) acquired them and installed a version of the bombsight in German bombers, Germany was no longer doing much bombing. The Battle of Britain—the German effort to bomb the British into submission—had failed, and the Germans were now having to devote most of the Luftwaffe's resources to the defense of Germany against Allied bombers.

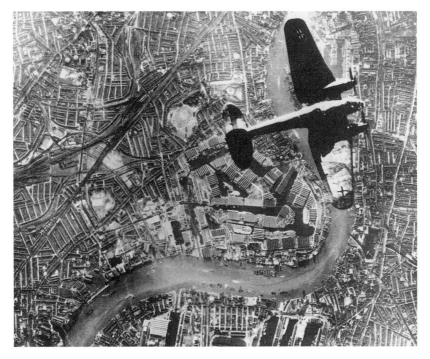

A German bomber attacks London at the height of the Battle of Britain in 1940. The photograph was made from another German bomber. (National Archives)

Lang, meanwhile, was arrested by the FBI, sent to jail for the rest of the war and then deported to Germany.

Colonel Erwin von Lahousen headed the Abwehr section that carried out sabotage operations. In 1942, his section launched Operation Pastorius, which had the aim of blowing up several American plants involved in making aluminum. Eight German agents traveled to the United States in two German submarines. Four of them were put ashore at Amagansett, a coastal town on Long Island east of New York City. The other group landed at St. Augustine in Florida.

The leader of the Amagansett group was Georg Dasch. On the trip across the Atlantic, he and another saboteur made up their minds that they could not work for Nazi Germany. (Dasch may have hoped that by exposing the plan, he would be able to keep the $160,000 that Lahousen had given the group to finance the sabotage.) On landing, therefore, they got word to the FBI of what was afoot. The FBI rounded up all the men. Dasch and his associate told the story of Pastorius at the trial of the saboteurs. With that testimony they saved their lives, receiving only prison sentences while the other saboteurs were executed.

Lahousen later claimed that he set up the mission under orders from Hitler. It was, he said, "the biggest blunder" made by the Abwehr sabotage arm.

Equally embarrassing to the Abwehr was the case of William G. Sebold. He was a German who became an American citizen. When he went back to Germany for a visit in 1939, the Abwehr recruited him and set him up as a radio operator in New York under the code name of Tramp. His reports came from several German spies in the United States.

Then, in 1941, the FBI arrested 33 people—among them Lang—as German spies. Nineteen of them came to trial in New York later that year. The star witness was Sebold. The prosecutor, United States Attorney Harold M. Kennedy, explained why. "For sixteen months," he told the jury, "the Federal Bureau of Investigation has been in constant communication with the Nazi secret service in Hamburg, Germany, by means of a shortwave station on Long Island, exchanging worthless 'information' about the American defense program for accurate reports on the activities of Nazi spies in this country. It was the German espionage system itself that had conceived the idea of a shortwave station here that would enable it to check on American defense preparations and at the same time regulate the activities of its secret agents in this country. The plan boomeranged because William G. Sebold betrayed the operation to agents of the FBI on his return from Germany early in 1940."

Kennedy's statement stands in contrast with the opinion voiced in 1937 by Erich Pheiffer, *V-Mann Leiter* (leader of agents) at the Abwehr station in Wilhelmshaven. "At every strategic point in the United States," he said, "we have at least one of our operatives. In every armament factory, in every shipyard in America we have a spy, several of them in key positions. The United States cannot plan a warship, design an airplane, develop a new device that we do not know of at once."

However accurate that statement might have been in 1937, it would not have stood up by the time the United States went to war with Germany in 1941. Part of the reason was that with the start of the war in Europe in 1939, Hitler ordered the Abwehr to soft- pedal its operations in the United States because he did not want to provoke the Americans into entering the war at that point. In addition, the FBI caught up with most of the spies sooner or later, and through some of them sent false or misleading information to Germany. Phillip Knightley, a British journalist who has written on espionage in World War II, has summed up the German effort in the United States this way: "German intelligence operations in the United States, spectacular though they may have appeared, were futile. Indeed, if the fact that some German agents were fed disinformation by the FBI is taken into account, Germany would probably have been better off with no spies in the United States at all."

***

Great Britain was the focus of a much more intense Abwehr effort. By 1940, the Germans had most of the countries in Europe under their control. Britain was the major enemy still standing, and German bombers were poised to begin the Battle of Britain to soften the British up for Operation Sealion—Hitler's planned invasion of the British Isles. Long before 1940, the Germans had made another kind of preparation by establishing spies and spy rings in the United Kingdom. The scope of this effort is suggested by the fact that at the start of the war, MI-5 had a list of nearly 400 people it suspected of being German agents.

In the prewar years, at least, the effort appears to have produced impressive results. The agents had compiled information on airfields, ports, harbor defenses, military posts, factories and mines throughout the British Isles. After the war, British counterintelligence agents going through surviving German documents found one entitled *Informationsheft Gross-Britannien*, which had been compiled in 1940 as part of the preparation for Sealion. It showed that the Germans had good information about the British intelligence service and the key people in it.

Much of that information came from a notable German intelligence coup, the Venlo incident. On the German side, the background to the incident was that Hitler wanted the SD to see what it could find out about the people and plans of the British SIS. On the British side, the aim was to see if members of the known opposition to Hitler in the Abwehr and the German army could be induced to overthrow Hitler and make peace with England.

Adolf Hitler (left), the German dictator, congratulates Heinrich Himmler on Himmler's 43rd birthday in 1943. Himmler, head of the hated SS (Schutzstaffel) and the domestic police, has been described as "the most cold-blooded and inhuman of all Nazi chiefs." (Library of Congress)

The first move was made by the Germans. Franz Fischer, a British SIS agent in Holland, told two other agents there— S. Payne Best and Richard Stevens—that he could put them in contact with a German opposition group. What the British did not know was that Fischer was a double agent who was also working with the SD.

Best and Stevens checked with London and got authority to proceed. They had a series of meetings with two Germans who went by the names of Captain Schaemmel and Captain Hausmann. (Schaemmel was in fact Walter Schellenberg, then head of the SD's section on foreign intelligence, and Hausmann was Max de Crinis, a psychologist at Berlin University.) By November 1939, matters had reached a stage where the two groups arranged to meet at a cafe in Venlo, a small village near the border between Germany and Holland. The Germans had promised to bring to the meeting a prominent opposition general. They had a man ready to play that part, too, but in the end he did not appear.

The reason he did not appear was that in the evening of November 8, the day before the meeting, a bomb went off at a beer cellar in Munich, shortly after Hitler had left. (It was known beforehand that Hitler would attend a celebration there of his first attempt to seize power 16 years earlier.) Hitler was convinced that the bombing was the result of a plot by the British secret service, and he ordered the SD to seize Best and Stevens at the Venlo meeting.

What happened at Venlo was described by Best after the war: "Schaemmel was standing on the veranda . . . and made a sign which I took to mean that our bird [the general] was inside . . . I stopped the engine and Stevens got out . . . There was a sudden noise of shouting and shooting. I looked up, and through the windscreen saw a large open car draw up . . . till our bumpers were touching. It seemed to be packed to overflowing with rough-looking men. Two were perched on the hood and were firing over our heads from submachine guns; others were standing up in the car and on the running boards; all shouting and waving pistols. Four men jumped off . . . and rushed towards us shouting: 'Hands up!'"

Best and Stevens were captured and carried across the border. Under interrogation they revealed a great deal of information about the British intelligence organization, providing the details that turned up later in *Informationsheft Gross-Britannien*.

The consequences of Venlo were far-reaching. On the German side, Canaris was made wary of making overtures to the British lest he get himself and the Abwehr in trouble with Hitler. On the British side, all future overtures from Germans opposed to Hitler were ignored or treated with great caution. Moreover, Churchill after becoming prime minister wrote a directive to the foreign secretary saying, "We do not desire to make any enquiries as to the terms of a peace with Hitler and . . . all our agents are strictly forbidden to entertain any such suggestions."

Another German success was the operation to which they gave the name *Nordpol* (North Pole), also calling it *Englandspiel* (England game) and including it in their *Funkspiel* (radio game). In 1942, Abwehr counterespionage agents picked up Hubert Lauwers, a Dutchman who was an agent and radio operator for the SOE. They had found him by what was known in the war as D/Fing or "deefing," meaning radio direction-finding. Lauwers had been sending information to London from other agents in Holland.

Major H. L. Giskes, the Abwehr's counterespionage chief in Holland, saw an opportunity to take advantage of the British. He persuaded Lauwers to continue sending radio messages, but under German control. Although Lauwers followed the German instructions, he tried to warn the British by leaving out of his messages the security check the SOE had given him. He even managed to get the word "caught" in one message without being detected.

The British, however, missed or ignored the warnings. Lauwers assumed they knew about his situation but were accepting it in order to carry out some counterstroke against the Germans, and so he went on sending the messages the Germans gave him.

In this way, the Germans effectively took control of SOE operations in Holland. Every time the British sent in agents or supplies, the Gestapo was there to capture them. One of the SOE radio operators (of 17 in all) controlled by the Abwehr would tell London that the operation had succeeded. And so the SOE believed it had a flourishing network of agents in Holland. It continued to send more agents and supplies. By the time the Germans wound up the operation on the eve of the Allied invasion of Europe in 1944, they had captured more than 50 agents and vast quantities of food, weapons and money that had been intended to help the Dutch resistance forces.

Canaris was considerably less successful, probably on purpose, in preparing for Operation Sealion. Hitler issued his order for the operation in September 1940, saying: "The task of the Army is to land strong forces in Southern England with the cooperation of the Navy and Air Force, to defeat the English Army and to occupy London. Other areas of England will be occupied as opportunity permits."

To prepare for the invasion, Canaris needed spies with special talents. They had to blend into the scene and be at hand when German invaders arrived in order to guide them and tell them what actions would be useful or harmful in a hostile countryside. Canaris did not have such a group in England. The ones he recruited were a ragtag lot, who received little training. The result was that the spies who actually made it to England were quickly captured.

One of them told at his trial some things about the training he received: "They gave me lessons in the structure of the English army—divisions and brigades—what they are formed of. What were important things to tell. For instance, where battalions were situated and how we could recognize them. Go to the café and listen, for soldiers always talk. As far as the RAF was concerned, they wanted to know where there were new aerodromes, where they put the new antiaircraft guns, how heavy and the exact position. What kind of planes were on the field and what number and which type."

The trials also revealed what the spies carried. Three of them who landed on the coast of Scotland in a small boat had in a suitcase a Mauser pistol, a radio set, two cardboard disks for setting up the radio code and a list of bomber and fighter stations in the eastern counties of England. The three men were arrested almost immediately because they were so conspicuously foreign.

General Ulrich Liss, head of the German army's intelligence operations, later reflected on the Sealion espionage operation. In other operations, he said, Canaris and the Abwehr had been "models of efficiency." In Sealion, although Canaris "appeared to be trying to be efficient, he was not doing his job against England with conviction." What Liss probably did not know was that Canaris was in league with the *Schwarze Kapelle* (Black Orchestra), a group of prominent Germans who tried repeatedly to overthrow Hitler or at least to thwart his soaring ambitions because they believed his policies would bring Germany to disaster. Hitler took a big step toward that disaster by invading Russia in June 1941.

Meanwhile, partly because the spy apparatus had failed to reveal how poorly prepared Britain was to withstand an invasion, he postponed Sealion. Soon he had so much on his hands in Russia that he could not hope to mount an invasion of England.

Canaris continued to see to it that the Allies got crucial information about German war plans. He was very careful about it, however, partly because of Venlo. Also because of Venlo, the British in particular were cautious about taking the information seriously.

By 1944, Hitler had become convinced that Canaris was not to be trusted. He ordered the SD to take over the Abwehr and moved Canaris to a meaningless job as head of Germany's economic warfare unit.

The effect of this reorganization was to put the German intelligence apparatus in disarray at a time when it should have been concentrating on the preparations of the Allies for their invasion of France. Abwehr agents, already hampered by nervousness about their future, were further handicapped because they received conflicting orders as the new intelligence headquarters tried to organize itself. The disarray in the German intelligence system also made it easier for the Allies to put over deceptions as they were preparing to give the Germans mistaken ideas about when and where the invasion would take place.

On receiving further evidence that Canaris had betrayed him, Hitler sent Schellenberg to arrest the former Abwehr chief in July 1944. Incarcerated in Flossenberg prison, Canaris worked out a code with the man in the next cell—Lieutenant Colonel H. M. Lunding, the former chief of the Danish secret service. On April 8, 1945, Canaris was charged with anti-Hitler acts and sentenced to death. That night he tapped out a message to Lunding: "I die for my country and with a clear conscience . . . I was only doing my duty to my country when I endeavored to oppose Hitler." The next day Canaris was executed by hanging. A month later, Germany surrendered, and the war in Europe ended.

Years after the war General James O. Curtis, an American who had been an intelligence officer at Allied headquarters in London during the war, discussed Canaris's activities with the author Anthony Cave Brown. Curtis said:

> I first heard the name Canaris in February 1944. My duties required me to check the authenticity of certain information reaching my desk. We had a system of grading information at SHAEF (Supreme Headquarters, Allied Expeditionary Force) which ranged from A1 to F6, so that the highest grade and most authentic information was graded A1 while the lowest grade and least authentic information was graded F6.
>
> It is not usual to get large amounts of A1 but I noticed that a surprising amount of A1 information was coming through. It was necessary for me to know the source, and so I inquired at a meeting of the Order of Battle intelligence section. A British officer, E. J. Foord, took me quietly on one side and said that the source was Canaris personally.

4

AMERICA TAKES THE PLUNGE
The Nation's First Centralized Intelligence

Reports began reaching Washington in the summer of 1943 that all was not well with OSS Detachment 101, the unit in Burma that was supporting resistance groups and gathering intelligence behind the Japanese lines. Code 109—known throughout the OSS as the identification for William J. Donovan—decided to see for himself. He arrived at detachment headquarters and was greeted by the commander, Colonel Carl Eifler. Shortly afterward, in the war room, he made a mildly critical remark about Eifler's work. What happened next was related by Richard Dunlop, who served with Detachment 101 and later wrote a biography of Donovan.

> Eifler fought down his anger. "Sir," he said, "would you like to go behind Jap lines and find out for yourself?" He knew he had thrown down a challenge Donovan could not refuse.
> Donovan smiled genially. "When do we leave?"
> "First thing in the morning, sir."
> As a rule even 101 men did not fly into the hidden bases in Burma, and yet Eifler was daring Donovan to do just that. Japanese Zeros (fighter planes) ruled the skies over Burma, and if Donovan, who carried the secrets of the Allied high command in his brain, were captured, it could be a disaster of staggering proportions.

Fly they did, though, in an elderly De Haviland Moth, with Eifler as the pilot and Donovan as the passenger. Donovan carried what OSS men called the L pill, which could be held under the tongue if danger seemed imminent. The capsule contained potassium cyanide. If you swallowed it intact, nothing happened, but if you chewed it and then swallowed, death followed swiftly. The plane made it to an advance base 150 miles behind the Japanese lines. Donovan inspected the base and was impressed. After a hairbreadth takeoff from the small landing strip, the plane made it safely back to headquarters. Donovan spent the evening playing bridge.

The episode was pure Donovan. OSS people everywhere knew that 109 might turn up at any time and would face any danger. They knew also that he would come with a flurry of ideas. As the OSS assessment staff put it, Donovan could "visualize an oak when he saw an acorn." The assessment continued:

> His imagination shot ahead, outflying days and distances, and where his imagination went, there would his body go soon afterward, and at every stop, brief as it might be, he would leave a litter of young schemes to be reared and fashioned by his lieutenants and transmuted finally into deeds of daring. This is the key . . . It explains why OSS undertook and carried out more different types of enterprises calling for more varied skills than any other single organization of its size in the history of our country.

Donovan, starting with nothing, first tapped a corps of experts on history, economics, geography and several other subjects. They were mostly college teachers, and they formed a branch that became known in OSS as "R&A" (for research and analysis). Their task was partly fact-finding (the research) and partly deciding how one fact related to another and what conclusion the facts pointed to (the analysis). Digging into atlases, business records, newspapers, picture files and many other sources, they built up a huge file of information on the places where American troops and ships might need to fight. By 1944, R&A staffs were operating not only at OSS headquarters in Washington but also in London, Algiers, Cairo, Caserta, Paris, Stockholm, New Delhi, Bari, Honolulu, Chungking, Bucharest, Istanbul, Rome, Lisbon and Athens.

Operation Torch, the Allied invasion of North Africa in 1942, benefited richly from the work of R&A. William J. Casey wrote that the scholars "delivered studies of the French North African railways, the capacity of the rolling stock, the condition of the roadbed and track, terrain maps, charts of reefs and channels, tidal tables—all assembled from manuals, engineering journals and other sources available in the Library of Congress." The result was that the invaders had "detailed information on what to expect at every landing point," along with maps of airports and seaports, the disposition of enemy ships and planes, up-to-the-minute weather reports and virtually everything else they might need to know.

Later in the war, R&A set up an economic objectives unit (EOU) to improve the method of choosing targets for Allied bombers sent over Germany. EOU studied the scene to identify industries that were crucial to the German economy. The result was to make ball-bearing, tire and engine factories the key targets and to pinpoint the times when a

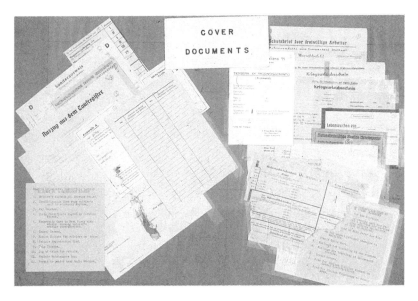

The OSS made false documents to provide cover stories for its spies and the agents it sent behind enemy lines. Several of the documents are shown here. (National Archives)

first attack should be followed by a second, just at the time when the factories were getting back into production.

Akin to R&A in name but not in function was R&D (research and development), which could be called the sly-tricks branch. It turned out the documents, clothes and other items OSS agents would need to establish and maintain their cover. R&D had sections for documents, camouflage and special assistance.

The documentation section set up a special engraving shop in Washington to produce fake papers. Whether the agent was going to Europe or the Far East, the shop turned out the appropriate passport, identity card, work permit, driver's license and other papers to make the agent seem to be what he claimed to be. An agent's life might depend on the apparent authenticity of his documents, and so the documentation section took great pains with them.

With equal attention to detail, the camouflage section provided other things an agent would need to look as though he belonged where he was. For example, a sharp counterespionage eye in occupied Norway could spot whether a man's clothes were sewn as though they had been made locally. The same was true of eyeglasses, dental work and such personal items as the agent's toothbrush, razor, briefcase and shoes.

Another specialty of the camouflage section was designing letter drops where agents could hide documents or pick up papers left there by a collaborator. The first effort used drops in the form of pieces of old wood that had been split and hollowed out so that a metal container could be inserted. The drops fell short of full success because some of them got picked up for firewood. The camouflage people decided that a drop had to be something that could not be burned or eaten. Thereafter they made drops that looked like stones or tin cans.

The spy also had to have a good cover story. OSS cooked up a typical one for an agent who was an American citizen of German descent but knew nothing about Germany except what his parents had told him. As briefed by OSS, he became a soldier who had been released, because of illness, from the German army, where he had been a clerk in headquarters of the 356th Infantry Division. He was heading for the south of Germany to recover his health in the mountains. The documentation section supplied him with proof: a German military pass with correct signatures; a hospital certificate of his illness, bearing the carefully forged signatures of a doctor in that hospital; a travel permit; and a series of photographs of himself, apparently taken over a period of time.

The special assistance section of OSS produced pills. One was the L capsule that Donovan carried on his dangerous flight in Burma. Another was the K pill, designed to knock out briefly the person to whom an agent gave it, say by slipping it into a drink, so that the agent could go through the victim's pockets or search his room. The TD pill was a truth tablet, designed to make sure the recipient told the truth under interrogation.

All these props and tools were designed to smooth the task of OSS spies. In recruiting spies, the OSS had a fairly easy task because of the large number of foreign-born or second-generation Americans in the country. OSS also was able to enlist many spies in countries occupied by Germany or Japan; they were people who had no love for the occupiers and welcomed a chance to work against them.

OSS paid great attention to the training of its agents. It set up several training schools, including one at the Congressional Country Club near Washington and another, known as "The Farm," on a 100-acre estate 20 miles away. Agents learned about cryptography, secret meetings with collaborators, tailing people without being spotted, searching rooms, handling explosives, using and maintaining weapons, interrogating captives, reading and drawing maps, means of defending themselves and many other useful things. They received code names and numbers.

Aline Griffith, who became an undercover agent in Spain, was "Tiger," code number 527. Tiger later married a Spanish nobleman and is now Aline, Countess of Romanones. A few years ago, she wrote about her experiences as an OSS agent and included an episode when she was sent to the south of Spain to meet an OSS contact named Blacky. Her mission was to give him some microfilm, which she carried taped to her waist, and a briefcase containing a radio and a Colt automatic pistol. Her chief gave her these instructions: "Tomorrow, at two-thirty P.M., in the back bench of the cathedral in the center of Málaga, Blacky will be seated with a white scarf around his neck. Kneel in the same pew for a few minutes. Pass him the briefcase and microfilm, if you are unobserved." She had some difficulties, but eventually she made it to the cathedral.

> A man entered the pew and knelt a short distance from me. He had a dirty white scarf around his neck. It all took place in a few moments. Without turning my head, I slid the gun wrapped in my silk scarf over the wooden bench. A hand reached out. A second later, my empty scarf was replaced. Then I pushed over the case containing the transmitter. Then I stretched out my upturned hand with the roll of microfilm in my open palm. I didn't even feel his touch as he removed it.

By the summer of 1942, the OSS had agents all over the world. As Donovan wrote in Life magazine after the war:

> OSS headquarters were established in every [war] theater, in England, North Africa, Switzerland and Sweden, from which we sent agents and guerrilla fighters into occupied France, Belgium, Holland, Germany, Austria, Yugoslavia and Italy—and on the other side of the globe we operated in Siam, China, Burma and Indochina. That was an effective wartime intelligence system. Information gatherers behind enemy lines, and scholars placed all the way from Washington to the front lines.

A major area of activity was France, where the OSS helped to organize and support French resistance groups, largely through three-man "Jedburgh" teams. (The name came from the Scottish town where they trained.) Each such hand-picked team consisted of an Englishman, an American and a Frenchman. The teams were intensively trained in weaponry, raiding and demolition tactics, radio work, silent movement and unarmed combat. Much of the lore of the OSS and many of its tales of heroism come from the work of the Jedburghs and similar guerrilla teams elsewhere.

The focus here, however, is on espionage. By the time of the Allied invasion of the European continent in June 1944, the OSS had close to 900 agents working in France, somewhat more than half of them French. Among other things, OSS people spotted in France a German division believed to be on the Russian front, thereby enabling the Allied command to shift weight against it and avoid an unpleasant surprise. An OSS team working at Le Bourget Airport near Paris was able to get hold of the plans of two secret war-production factories, one making explosives and the other turning out oil for submarines and airplanes. Allied bombers destroyed both of them.

A peculiar problem that came up in equipping OSS agents for work in France was making sure they had paper money that would pass as French. OSS knew, and so did the occupying Germans, that only banks and government agencies got fresh and unmutilated money. A person found with new money would immediately be suspected. In addition, French banks traditionally counted paper money on receiving it and then pinned the notes together into small packets with common pins. In order to pass, therefore, the money given to OSS agents needed aging and pinholing.

Pinholing was easy enough, but aging presented a problem. The money could not be aged with ordinary garden dirt because the soil left a characteristic residue that could be detected easily by Germans stopping an agent on suspicion. Eventually, OSS found that the best way to age new bills was to scatter them around the floor of a busy office. Over a period of hours, the workers walking about on their regular business would scuff the notes enough to make them look suitably aged.

Operation Anvil, the Allied invasion of southern France in August 1944, represented a big payoff for OSS efforts in both spying and deceiving the enemy. (In this operation as in others in Europe, OSS worked in league with the British.) The information supplied by agents in France was so detailed that the Allied commanders knew the condition and location of the German defenders down to the last pillbox.

The deception effort was aimed at making the Germans think the attack would come at Marseilles rather than farther east at Toulon. There was no way to conceal the fact that a fleet of some 1,200 ships was approaching France from Italy and North Africa. The question for the Germans was where the ships were heading. To provide a misleading answer, the Allies flew near Marseilles before dawn on the day of the invasion and dropped a population of rubber dummies fitted with parachutes that opened automatically. It appeared to be a paratroop attack. A little later, a group of transport planes flew over the same area and dropped a hail of strips of wide tinfoil. German radar read the event as an approaching fleet of enemy aircraft. At the same time, a small fleet of PT boats, which were really only large motorboats, scurried toward the French coast. German radar read the event as an approaching enemy naval fleet. A few hours later, the real invasion began at places where the Germans had had no warning. The invasion was a success, and the Allied forces rapidly advanced northward through France, soon joining the forces that had invaded Normandy in June and were rolling eastward across France.

France was only one of many countries where the OSS was active. In neutral Sweden, for example, the Harvard professor Bruce Hopper ran an operation that gave the Allies valuable information on Germany at a time when such information was hard to get. One of his recruits was Erik Erikson, a Swedish businessman. In a plot hatched by the OSS, Erikson let it be known that he intended to set up a plant in Sweden to make synthetic oil. In this role he went to another Swede, August Rosterg, who was the principal owner of a German synthetic-oil firm. Rosterg plied Erikson with much useful information on how Germany was doing in refining and importing oil. He also arranged in late 1944 for Erikson to take a guided tour of synthetic-oil plants in Germany. This eye in the enemy's heartland spotted things of great use when Allied bombers attacked the plants. Erikson's feats were later made into a movie, *The Counterfeit Spy*, starring William Holden.

Hopper's operation in Stockholm also managed to tighten the noose on Germany's supply of ball bearings at a time when Allied bombers had wreaked havoc on Germany's own ball-bearing factories, and Germany was depending on Sweden to sustain the supply. Since the Swedes were supposed to be neutral, the Allies could hope to block this supply if they could get enough information about it to convince Sweden that the traffic was unwise. Hopper recruited a shipping clerk in one of the main plants of SKF, Sweden's leading manufacturer of ball bearings. With the detailed information obtained from the clerk about shipments of bearings and ball-bearing machinery to Germany, the Allies convinced the Swedish government to stop the traffic.

The OSS chief in Switzerland, a neutral country right in the middle of the war in Europe, was Allen Dulles, later head of the Central Intelligence Agency. Operating out of a house at 23 Herren Street in Bern, he scored several intelligence triumphs.

One of his greatest triumphs resulted from a British mistake. In August 1943, Fritz Kolbe of the German Foreign Office walked unannounced into the British legation in Bern. He asked to see Colonel Henry Cartwright, the military attaché, who also worked for MI-9. That was the British intelligence arm that helped people escape from Germany and took down their stories.

Kolbe said he opposed the Nazis and therefore would be willing to turn crucial Foreign Office documents over to the Allies. Cartwright was suspicious. He knew the Abwehr had been trying to plant somebody in his office, and he decided that Kolbe must be the plant. He rejected the offer.

Kolbe then turned to Dulles, who was impressed by what he had to offer. Dulles gave Kolbe the code name of George Woods. Over the next 16 months, Kolbe delivered more than

1,500 secret Foreign Office papers to Dulles. The papers revealed the cable traffic between the Foreign Office and German diplomatic posts all over the world.

Some of the traffic included messages from the German military and air attachés in Tokyo, providing the Allies with useful information on the enemy in the Far East. Dulles later described how he got word to Kolbe late in the war, when the focus of the war effort was turning to the Far East, that more information on Japan would be helpful. Dulles and Kolbe had made an arrangement for emergency communication based on an imaginary girlfriend of Kolbe's who lived in Switzerland. Dulles, referring to Kolbe as "the source," related how the arrangement worked in this case.

Little is left of the German synthetic oil plant at Zetz after an attack by Allied bombers in 1945. The OSS office in Sweden engineered a guided tour of German synthetic oil plants for an agent in 1944 with the aim of choking off this vital source of German oil supplies. By April 1945, the Allies had cut German oil supplies to 7.5 percent of normal. (Library of Congress)

Since postcards seem more innocent to the censor than sealed letters, the "girl friend" sent to the source's home in Berlin a beautiful postal card of the Jungfrau. "She" wrote on it that a friend of hers in Zurich had a shop which had formerly sold Japanese toys but had run out of them and couldn't import them because of wartime restrictions; in view of the close relations between Germany and Japan, couldn't he help her out by suggesting where in Germany she could buy Japanese toys for her shop? My source got the point immediately, since he knew all the messages from the Swiss "girl friend" were from me. The next batch of cables from the German Foreign Office which he sent me were largely from German officials in the Far East and told of the plight of the Japanese navy and air force.

Summarizing the entire Kolbe story after the war, Dulles wrote that Kolbe "turned in to us some of the best technical and tactical information on the V-weapons, on the effects of Allied bombings, on German planning, on the gradually weakening fabric of the whole Nazi regime." Kolbe, Dulles said, "was not only our best source on Germany but undoubtedly one of the best secret agents any intelligence service has ever had."

Dulles also had a highly valuable contact in Hans Gisevius, an Abwehr officer in Switzerland. Gisevius was a founder of the Schwarze Kapelle and a member of Canaris's inner circle, and his role in Switzerland was to set up a Canaris-Donovan contact through Dulles. Among other things, Gisevius tipped off the Americans and British through Dulles that the Germans had solved the codes used by the American and British ambassadors in Switzerland. The tip cut off a valuable source of information for the Nazis—information that had kept them somewhat up to date on the activities of the Schwarze Kapelle because of that group's ties with Leland Harrison, the American minister to Switzerland. And Gisevius, as Donovan told President Truman after the war in Europe had ended, "supplied early information on the preparation of the V-1 and V-2 bombs, which in conjunction with other sources led to the identification of Peenemünde as the Germans' proving ground for the new weapons." The result was a heavy Allied bombing attack on Peenemünde in August 1943, which severely disrupted the V-weapon program.

Another source Dulles had was the Abwehr man in Zurich. Without giving his name, Dulles tells a story about how the man had dinner with him at the Herren Street house one night and got in trouble because his initials were in his hat. Dulles's cook, who turned out to be a German spy ("a better cook than a spy," Dulles said) heard them speaking German and reported to her Nazi contact that a man with certain initials had been visiting Dulles. The Nazis confronted the man, but he faced them down by telling them that he was acting on orders from Canaris, that Dulles was an important source of intelligence for Germany and that if they breathed a word of all this to Berlin, they would lose their jobs. He got away with it. "Everybody learned a lesson from this," Dulles wrote, "I that my cook was a spy; my German contact that he should remove his initials from his hat; and all of us that attack is the best defense and that if agent A is working with agent B, one sometimes never knows until the day of judgment who, after all, is deceiving whom."

Late in the war, after the Allies had recaptured France, Dulles was in Paris for a meeting with Donovan. He was staying at the Hotel Ritz. One night he was heading for his room when a stranger came up to him and said, "I beg of you, where is 110?" Dulles later wrote: "I have to explain that in the OSS we all had code numbers . . . which we used in secret communications. If the messages were intercepted, at least the identity of the persons mentioned therein could not become known. Since we had occasion to use these numbers practically every day in incoming and outgoing messages, they became attached to us in our minds very much like a name. I was 110 . . ." The stranger's question caught Dulles off guard. "I was just about to say, 'You're talking to him. I'm 110,' when I suddenly woke up to the reality of the situation. He was lost in the badly lighted corridors of the hotel and was looking for his room, which happened to be 110."

Dulles also was a key figure in Operation Sunrise (Churchill called it Crossword). In this endeavor he had the help of Gero Gaevernitz, a German-born businessman who had become an American citizen. Gaevernitz had business interests in Switzerland and good connections with the anti-Hitler movement in Germany. With his help Dulles carried out a series of complex negotiations with the German generals Karl Wolf and Heinrich von Vietinghoff in Italy. The operation led to the first German capitulation of the war—the surrender of German forces in Italy on May 2, 1945. It spared the Allies hard last-ditch fighting against the large German army in Northern Italy and paved the way for the final German surrender a few days later.

Toward the end of the war, OSS began to make some scores in Germany itself. In December 1944, only four OSS agents were inside Germany; when the war ended the following May, there were more than 150. Many of them were Germans who had been made prisoners of war by the Allies. If their records and interviews showed them to be anti-Nazi, they made good recruits for the OSS.

The new recruit signed a contract with the OSS and was taken to a safe house (known to OSS people as a "Joe") to be fitted out and trained. Casey describes part of the preparation:

> The agent was given the dog tag every German soldier wore around his neck, his pay book, travel orders, train tickets and ration stamps. All of them were carefully crafted to dovetail with his new identity. A visit to our lovingly built-up stock of German uniforms and other paraphernalia followed. The agent would get a uniform, have his picture taken to complete the documentation process and would rehearse the cover story until he could blurt it out when awakened from a deep sleep.

The agents were parachuted into Germany with a newly developed tool that turned out to be invaluable. It was Joan Eleanor, or J/E, a compact, battery-operated radio or wireless telephone that the agent could use to communicate with an OSS plane flying near him.

Casey, who by this time was head of the OSS headquarters in London, had drawn up a priority list of the information the Allies wanted from the agents in Germany. First on the list were troop movements behind the battle lines, so that Allied commanders could have notice of German defensive moves as the Allied attack moved into Germany. Next was identification of targets for bombing. Third was information on war-production plants. Finally, the agents were to look for groups in Germany that might resist the Nazis and for plans by the Nazis for postwar resistance.

The input from three teams indicates the kind of information the agents produced. Team Hammer in Berlin picked up key points about the city's transportation network and the places where bombs could disrupt it. The same team discovered an electric power plant that was still running in spite of Allied bombing and was supplying power to keep several war plants running; it was bombed again. The Luxe I team in Bavaria found a factory making jet fighter planes in a highway tunnel and turned in useful information on troop movements and defense arrangements. Team Pickaxe near Munich reported on rail and road traffic and troop movements. One report of heavy troop movements brought about a bombing of the rail center within 12 hours.

During all this time, other branches of the OSS were hard at work. The Intelligence Photographic Documentation Project began building up a collection of aerial photographs on areas of strategic importance in Europe and the Far East. The photographs covered coastlines, port facilities and major military installations.

Back in Washington, the Morale Operations arm of the OSS was busy conducting a war of rumors. There was the confusion rumor: The German mint is printing large amounts of currency; life insurance companies in Germany are going broke because of the large number of deaths. There was the personal gossip rumor: Hitler will appear here or there—and when he didn't, the suggestion was made that he was ill or dead. (These rumors worked so well that the German propaganda minister, Josef Goebbels, put out a story on Radio Berlin that he had originated them in order to "lull the Allies into complacency and set them up for the winter offensive.") And there was the pipe-dream rumor: German soldiers who let themselves be captured would be given good jobs with the Allies.

Quite another area of activity was the array of dirty tricks thought up by Stanley Lovell and his Research and Development section. Lovell was a businessman, chemist and inventor from New England. Donovan, at their first meeting, said he wanted Lovell to be the Professor Moriarty of the OSS, referring to the evil genius in the Sherlock Holmes stories by A. Conan Doyle. "I need every subtle device and every underhanded trick to use against the Germans and the Japanese—by our own people—but especially by the underground resistance groups in all occupied countries," Donovan said.

One of Lovell's devices was a special shoe in which the bottom filler between the inner and outer soles, normally made of ground cork and wax, consisted of paper or cloth bearing messages. "No inspection of that shoe, short of literally cutting it all apart, could expose the fact that it contained a surprisingly large quantity of information," Lovell wrote.

Then there was "Hedy," a firecracker device that made a noise like a falling bomb followed by a loud explosion when a wire loop was pulled to set it off. It was made for spies in tight spots who needed something to cause a moment of panic so they could create a diversion in order to pull off some trick or get away. Lovell said he named the device for the beautiful actress Hedy Lamarr "because my lusty young officers said she created panic wherever she went."

Another device was the "anerometer," a fuse that worked by barometric pressure. Packed with an explosive in a length of garden hose and sneaked aboard an airplane, it would go off when the plane reached an altitude of 5,000 feet. Lovell remarked that OSS people blew up many German and Japanese planes with this device.

If the target was a train, Lovell's people offered "Casey Jones." It was a small container with a magnet on one side and an electric eye on the other. The magnet held the container to the steel underside of a railroad car, and the electric eye set off an explosive when the train entered the darkness of a tunnel. The explosive would then derail the train. Because the "accident" happened in a tunnel, the people who were sent to restore service were delayed by the cramped conditions and poor light. The "limpet," attached to the hull of a ship below the waterline, would blow a hole in the hull after salt water had eaten away a magnesium-alloy window on the device. For roads and runways there was a small piece of steel with four prongs. No matter how it landed, three prongs stuck up, guaranteeing to cause a flat tire on any vehicle or airplane that ran over it. Since the devices were scattered in large numbers, the likelihood was that the vehicle would wind up with all its tires flat and badly cut up.

***

The war ended and the OSS disbanded. Donovan went back to his law practice and his numerous other interests. By 1957, however, it was evident that he was not well. The diagnosis was brain disease. The trouble, made worse by a series of strokes, soon rendered him severely incapacitated. He died early in 1959. President Dwight D. Eisenhower, who had been Allied commander in Europe during the war and knew Donovan well, said on hearing of the death: "What a man! We have lost the last hero."

5

THE WILY BRITISH
Lessons in Spying and Deception

In the summer of 1939, an unexpected letter reached the desk of Hector Boyes, the naval attaché at the British embassy in Oslo. Although it was written in flawless German, it carried a Norwegian postmark. The signature was, "A well-wishing German scientist." There was no other identification. The letter said that the writer was in a position to tell the British what the Germans were doing in several areas of science and technology. If the British were interested, they should make a slight change in the standard opening of one of their regular news broadcasts in German.

The British made the change, and early in September, a package of modest size arrived at the Oslo embassy. It held several typewritten pages and a sealed box. The sealed box contained what turned out to be a proximity fuse, designed to make an anti- aircraft shell explode when it came near a solid object (presumably the airplane it had been aimed at). The typewritten pages described the fuse and told how it worked. They also reported on two types of German radar, which had the code names Freya and Wurzburg, on rocket-propelled bombs being developed at Peenemünde in Germany and on a radio-beam system for blind bombing, code-named Knickebein.

The naval attaché sent the package to London. The military services and most of the people in MI-6 studied the material and eventually decided it must be a hoax. They came to that conclusion partly because the Venlo incident that fall made them suspicious of every German overture and partly because few military or intelligence people were quite prepared for the extent to which the war would turn on developments in science and technology.

Fortunately, Stewart Menzies sent the Oslo Report (as it soon came to be known) to R. V. Jones, who had recently been assigned to work part time with MI-6 as its scientific adviser. Jones took the report seriously, knowing how good the Germans were at science and technology and how hard they were working in those areas. A test of the proximity fuse quickly confirmed his view; it showed the fuse to be better than anything the British had developed. As time went on, one item after another in the Oslo Report turned out to be real. (Jones said later that "in the few dull moments of the War I used to look up the Oslo Report to see what should be coming along next.") And the report proved to be one of the pivotal intelligence documents of the war.

British intelligence operated through several arms. Often more than one of them was involved in a particular operation. MI-6 was the main arm, and some of its main successes came through the work of Jones and his associates. Other arms included MI-5, the Special Operations Executive (SOE), the XX Committee and LCS, the London Controlling Section.

Menzies, unlike Donovan, headed an old and practiced organization. Aware of the intelligence weakness in the United States, he moved early in the war to establish an arm of MI-6 there to nudge the Americans—who were officially neutral in the war until the Japanese attack on Pearl Harbor—toward the British side. Menzies's move was the origin of BSC (British Security Coordination), code name Intrepid, headed by William Stephenson. BSC set up headquarters in Room 3603 of Rockefeller Center in New York. Within a year, Stephenson had built up a network of some 3,000 agents, and the hand of Intrepid appeared in many places.

One of them was Times Square in New York. Early on a March morning in 1941, a taxi swerved from its path on Seventh Avenue, struck a pedestrian crossing the square at 43rd Street and sped away. A black sedan following the taxi then ran over the fallen man and just as quickly disappeared from the scene. When the police arrived, the man was dead.

Papers identified the victim as Julio Lopez Lido. The police viewed the incident as a hit-and-run accident. Within a few days, however, the FBI began looking into the matter. FBI agents had seen a letter intercepted by a BSC outpost in Bermuda that checked telegrams and air mail between the United States and Europe for signs of German spies and sympathizers. In the letter, a German spy described the "accident" in terms indicating that Lido was important to the Germans.

The FBI went to Stephenson, believing BSC to have had a hand in the incident. He was a bit reluctant, because his information about the man had come from a secret source BSC had in the German consulate in New York. "Lido," Stephenson said, was in fact Ulrich von der Osten, the head of a German spy ring in the United States. The taxi and the sedan had "eliminated" him. On the basis of the information from Stephenson, the FBI soon rounded up von der Osten's entire network of spies.

Intrepid's hand also appeared in the work of "Cynthia." She was Amy Thorpe, an American married to a British diplomat. When they were stationed in Poland, she had done valuable work for MI-6 in getting information about Enigma, the German code machine. Stephenson knew of that feat and recruited her to work for BSC in the United States. He gave her the code name Cynthia and arranged for her to rent a house in Washington, D.C.

Cynthia was good at cultivating friendships with important men. Her first triumph in the United States was to obtain the Italian naval code through her friendship with Admiral Alberto Lais at the Italian embassy. With the aid of that weapon, the Royal Navy soon trounced the Italian fleet near

Greece—a feat that Churchill said ended "all challenge to British naval mastery in the eastern Mediterranean at this critical time."

Stephenson then assigned Cynthia the task of getting the French naval code from the French embassy in Washington. The British wanted it because they suspected the Vichy government of France (which the Germans had set up after overrunning the country) of giving the Germans information about ship convoys leaving the United States for England and about British naval and merchant vessels that were being repaired in American ports.

Cynthia set out to cultivate the press secretary of the embassy, Charles Brousse. He was reluctant to help her at first, but then he saw an order from Vichy for information on British ships in American dockyards. He assumed the information would be passed on to the Germans, and he wanted no part of that.

With some effort, which included doping the security guard at the embassy, Brousse arranged for Cynthia to get to the code books in the embassy safe. They had the help of a safecracker on loan from the OSS—a man who had been let out of prison to contribute his skills at safecracking to the war effort. In the dead of night, Cynthia and Brousse handed the code books out the window of the embassy to a BSC man. He had them photographed and returned them to the embassy, so that by morning they were back in the safe. The code helped the British stay ahead of the moves of the French fleet (now under German control through the Vichy government) during the planning for Operation Torch, the Allied invasion of North Africa in 1942. After the war, Cynthia married Brousse.

Stephenson also was the driving force behind Camp X near Toronto, the training ground for many American and British spies, saboteurs and counterespionage agents. Among other things, Camp X had areas that looked like Hollywood sets, duplicating sections of European cities where the trainees might be working. It was at Camp X, too,

Dummy American military vehicles in an English town serve to trick German aerial reconnaissance. Inflatable dummies of this kind were developed at Camp X in Canada, where American and British secret agents were trained. (U.S. Army Intelligence and Security Command)

that the magician Jasper Maskelyne developed inflatable shapes that, when they were filled with air, looked like tanks, trucks and guns. Inflated and set about on the ground, these dummies served later to deceive the Germans about the size and position of Allied forces.

One of the first deceptions practiced by the British actually had a basis in fact. As part of their effort to defend their coast against a German invasion, they laid pipes along the beach at Dover. The pipes had holes at intervals. When fuel was pumped through the pipes and lit, the beach flamed right down to the water line. Although it produced a forbidding sight, the scheme could not have been extended very far except at great expense.

John Baker White, a young major in the military intelligence department concerned with psychological warfare, saw this setup in the summer of 1940, when British concern about a German invasion was at its height. It was, he said, "a frightening spectacle, with clouds of thick, blinding black smoke through which shot great jets of red flame."

Baker White decided that more could be made of this idea than the facts justified. His plan was to lead the Germans to believe that the British were capable of "setting the sea on fire," as he put it, creating a ring of flame along the coast so that invading soldiers would have to wade through burning water. He put the rumor out through British agents in places where he knew the Abwehr would pick it up.

Before long it was clear that the Germans had swallowed the story and were trying to devise ways of getting troops through the burning sea. The story gained momentum when the bodies of some 40 German soldiers washed up on the British coast. They were from a group that had been practicing for the invasion in barges that sank. Churchill wrote later: "This was the source of a widespread rumour that the Germans had attempted an invasion and had suffered very heavy losses either by drowning or by being burnt in patches of sea covered with flaming oil. We took no steps to contradict these tales, which spread freely through the occupied countries in a widely exaggerated form, and gave much encouragement to the oppressed populations." The tales may also have contributed to Hitler's decision to postpone Operation Sealion; at least there were reports from Germany that he was concerned over the prospect that his troops might have to advance through a burning sea.

***

Among the leading oppressors of the populations in the occupied countries, as well as of Germans suspected of opposition to Hitler, was Reinhard Heydrich. As head of the SD, he had been ruthless in suppressing anti-Nazi figures in Germany and in killing opposition leaders in occupied Poland. He was also maneuvering slyly to enlarge the SD's intelligence activity at the expense of the Abwehr.

By 1941, Heydrich appeared to be threatening the position of Canaris. That was troublesome to MI-6, which was finding Canaris to be helpful in many ways. Menzies decided that Heydrich should be eliminated.

By that time Heydrich was in Czechoslovakia, supervising the Nazi occupation. Colin Gubbins of SOE chose two men from the Czechoslovakian army in exile, Josef Gabcik and Jan Kubis, to carry out the assassination. Gubbins sent them to Camp X for training. There they practiced in movielike sets made to resemble parts of Prague, where Heydrich had his headquarters. By the end of the year, SOE had delivered the two men to Czechoslovakia, where they waited for their chance to strike.

The chance came in March. A clock in Heydrich's office was not working right, and a secretary called a Czech worker in to fix it. He spotted on the desk a sheet of paper setting out exactly where Heydrich would be from hour to hour on March 27. The repairman saw to it that the information got to the assassins, and on the fateful day they took up a position on a curve that Heydrich's car was due to pass. The car appeared. Gabcik stepped into the road and aimed his submachine gun at Heydrich. The gun failed to go off. Heydrich and his driver stood up in the open car and shot Gabcik just as Kubis tossed a grenade into the car.

The explosion wounded Heydrich, but at first it seemed as though he would recover. For more than two months he lay in a hospital, and then he died.

The British thrust against Heydrich removed one of the most powerful enemy leaders and provided some breathing room for Canaris and the *Schwarze Kapelle*, but at great cost to people other than the British. In retaliation for the assassination of Heydrich, the Germans arrested nearly 10,000 people in Prague and killed some 1,500 of them. Then, suspecting that the people in the village of Lidice were hiding the assassins, the Germans rounded up everybody in the place. They shot all the males aged 16 or more and carried off the women and children. Then they wiped out the vacant buildings by fire and dynamite.

In the preparations for Operation Torch, the invasion of North Africa, MI-6 had three main tasks. One was to keep track of the activity of the German U-boats (submarines) in the North Atlantic so that convoys building up supplies for Torch could avoid them. Another was to protect the Allied cover plans, which sought to convince the Germans that the attack would come in any of several places except North Africa. A third was to find out what the Germans thought the Allies would do, so as to see if the cover plans were working.

Most of MI-6's successes in these areas came from breaking the German codes. Menzies then had the problem of making sure the Germans did not realize that the uncanny ability of the Allies to intercept German ships supplying the defenders in North Africa resulted from deciphering their codes. He dealt with the problem by having the word put out that the information on German shipping came from Italian spies. Hitler had a low opinion of the skill and helpfulness of his Italian allies anyway, and the stories leaked by MI-6 sounded more likely to him than the notion that the British could read the secret German code traffic.

Operation Torch was the first great Allied success of the war. It succeeded largely because the choking off of supplies to the German troops in North Africa left them weak and unable to maneuver successfully.

The next step in the Allied plan was Operation Husky, an invasion of Sicily to establish a base for attacking Italy and southern France. Sicily was as obvious a target to the Germans as to the Allies, and so again the Allies wanted to deceive Hitler into thinking the attack would come somewhere else. The main scheme for doing that came from Ewen Montagu, an officer in British naval intelligence. His plan, carried out by LCS and the XX Committee under the code name Operation Mincemeat, was one of the memorable deceptions of the war.

The plan was to obtain a body and fit it out as a British officer carrying secret documents indicating that the next moves by the Allies would be in Sardinia and Greece, with a feint toward Sicily. The officer, appearing to have been killed in a plane crash in the Mediterranean, was to be floated ashore near Huelva in southern Spain. The Abwehr had an agent there, and the Spanish government usually cooperated with the Germans, so it was a good bet that the Germans would soon hear about the documents.

With some difficulty, LCS got the body of a young man who had died of pneumonia. Given the identity of William Martin, acting major in the Royal Marines, and false documents to prove it, the body was launched from the submarine *Seraph* in April 1943. Chained to it, indicating that the officer was the bearer of important papers, was a briefcase containing a letter from General Sir Harold Alexander, commander of British forces in North Africa. The letter laid out the "plan" for attacks in places other than Sicily.

Sure enough, the body of "Major Martin" reached Spanish authorities. They turned the documents over to the Germans, who photographed them and put them back in the briefcase, which the Spanish then turned over to the British, making it look as though it had not been opened. The copies went to Berlin. On May 12, Hitler issued a directive saying the Allies could be expected to attack again soon in the Mediterranean and sending troops to the areas "most endangered: in the Western Mediterranean, the Peleponese and Dodecanese islands." As General Lord Ismay put it later, the directive "spread-eagled the German defensive effort right across Europe." In July, the Allies attacked Sicily. The German were spread too thin, and the attack succeeded easily. After the war, Montagu told the story of Operation Mincemeat in a famous book, *The Man Who Never Was.*

(Mincemeat, Husky and Torch were among hundreds of code names employed by the Allies during the war. It was characteristic of Churchill to think about this detail among the many other things he had on his mind. In August 1943, he wrote a memorandum on the subject. "I have crossed out on the attached paper many unsuitable names. Operations in which large numbers of men may lose their lives ought not to be described by code-words which imply a boastful and overconfident sentiment, such as 'Triumphant,' or conversely, which are calculated to invest the plan with an air of despondency, such as 'Woebetide,' 'Massacre,' 'Jumble,' 'Trouble,' 'Fidget,' 'Flimsy,' Pathetic,' and 'Jaundice.' They ought not to be names of a frivolous character, such as 'Bunnyhug,' 'Billingsgate,' 'Aperitif,' and 'Ballyhoo . . .' Care should be taken in all this process. An efficient and a successful administration manifests itself equally in small as in great matters.")

Meanwhile, back in London, Menzies and MI-6 were concerned about getting information on the Atlantic Wall, the system of fortifications Hitler was building along the west-

One of the great deceptions by the Allies during the war was Operation Mincemeat, which sought to convince the Germans that Sicily was not the next target of invasion in 1943. The deception succeeded in spreading the German defenses widely along the Mediterranean coast. The invasion of Sicily, seen here shortly after Allied landing boats had reached the shore, was a success and established a base for the later invasions of Italy and southern France. (Library of Congress)

Hitler's Atlantic Wall, built to defend occupied France against the Allied invasion of 1944, was known in detail by the invading forces because of work by spies and interceptions of German messages by Ultra and Magic. A section of the wall is shown in this German photograph. (Library of Congress)

ern coast of France in anticipation of an Allied attack there. One of the best networks MI-6 had in France was Jade Amicol. (Each MI-6 network in France got a name derived from a precious stone together with the code name of the leader—in this case two leaders, L'Amiral and Le Colonel, whose names were abbreviated and combined.) Jade Amicol's main operation, never found by the Germans, was in a convent in Paris. A radio installed over the sacristy was the chief means of communication between Paris and MI-6, and the convent also collected secret mail for MI-6.

One day René Duchoz, a painter and paperhanger who belonged to a group connected with Jade Amicol, saw a notice put out in Caen by the German engineering group building the Atlantic Wall. The notice asked for bids on work in the group's headquarters. Duchoz went into the headquarters and found that one of the jobs was wallpapering the office of the head man. Making an attractively low bid, he got the job. The head man then left the office to go to a meeting, and Duchoz set about doing some preparatory work. Noticing a pile of maps on the desk, he looked at the top one and found that it was the blueprint for a key section of the Atlantic Wall. He took it and hid it behind a mirror. Apparently no one noticed that it was gone, probably because the head man went out of town for a few days. When Duchoz returned to do the wallpapering, the map was still behind the mirror. It went out of the building with him that day, rolled up in some wallpaper, and soon reached the convent. L'Amiral himself flew this great intelligence prize to MI-6 headquarters in London.

MI-6 seems also to have had a hand in the strange goings-on at the British embassy in Istanbul, the capital of Turkey and a hotbed of espionage activity by both sides in the war. There the British ambassador, a man with the splendid name of Sir Hughe Montgomery Knatchbull-Hugessen, had a valet named Elyesa Bazna. One day in 1943, Bazna turned up at the home of Albert Jenke, an official of the German embassy in Istanbul. Bazna said he had been stealing and photographing secret documents passing between Sir Hughe and the British Foreign Office in London. He offered to sell the photographs to the Germans.

Word of this offer soon reached the German ambassador in Istanbul, Franz von Papen. He asked Berlin what to do, and Berlin said to go ahead. Papen gave Bazna the code name Cicero, and over a period of several months Cicero supplied photographs of what looked like top-secret British documents to the Germans. For these apparent plums, they paid him some 300,000 British pounds, then equivalent to about $1.2 million.

It was not long before people began reporting to London that the Germans had a spy in Sir Hughe's embassy. Among them was Allen Dulles, who learned about Cicero from his contact Fritz Kolbe in the German Foreign Office and reported it to Count Vanden Huyvel, the MI-6 chief in Switzerland. Dulles wrote after the war that three days later, "Vanden Huyvel came to my office and quite literally begged me to forget about the telegrams [from Kolbe] and to take no action whatsoever about the Cicero case . . . Count Vanden Huyvel said London was 'aware' of the case and, while Vanden Huyvel did not say so, it was obvious to me that the British were playing some sort of game with Cicero."

The game apparently was to help convince Hitler that the Allies would attack in the Balkan region as well as in France. It succeeded, with other efforts along the same line, in making him hold in the Balkans some 25 divisions that he might otherwise have deployed against the attack in France.

Years later, Menzies was asked about this case. he replied, "Of course Cicero was under our control." Bazna, who left his job in the British embassy thinking he was a rich man, quickly ran into trouble with the Turkish police. They had discovered that the British banknotes he spent so freely were counterfeit. The notes were from a large supply the Sicherheitsdienst had printed to finance its espionage moves.

***

Many of the British scores in the intelligence effort came in the new area of science and technology, largely thanks to the work of R. V. Jones and his associates. Churchill called their area of activity "the wizard war," a term Jones used as the title of a book he wrote about the work after the war. "This was a secret war," Churchill wrote, "whose battles were lost or won unknown to the public; and only with difficulty is it comprehended, even now [1949], by those outside the small high scientific circles concerned. No such warfare had ever been waged by mortal men. The terms in which it could be recorded or talked about were unintelligible to ordinary folk. Yet if we had not mastered its profound meaning and used its mysteries, even while we saw them only in the glimpse, all the efforts, all the prowess of the fighting airmen, all the bravery and sacrifices of the people, would have been in vain."

One of the first triumphs in the wizard war involved what Jones called the Battle of the Beams. The Germans had developed three systems of radio beams (Knickebein, Wotan

I and Wotan II) to direct their bombers to target areas in England. Jones worked out the characteristics of the systems and devised means of jamming the beams so that they were ineffective or sent the bombers to the wrong places. He had a similar achievement with Freya and Wurzburg, the German radar systems on the coast of France, thereby crippling the German scheme for getting early warning of Allied bomber fleets heading for Germany. (In a commando raid engineered by Jones on the French coastal area known as Bruneval, the British actually seized a Wurzburg apparatus and brought it back to England.)

Jones also made MI-6 aware of the possibility that the Germans might be developing an atomic bomb. The Oslo Report had revealed that they were doing atomic research. Through Norwegian sources MI-6 learned that the Germans, having occupied Norway, were depending on the Vemork hydroelectric plant near Oslo for their supply of heavy water, which was crucial to the operation of atomic reactors. Norwegian agents got the plans of the plant for MI-6, and late in 1942 the British mounted Operation Freshman, a paratroop attack on the plant. The attackers failed to reach their target.

SOE undertook the next move. They built a large model of the plant and practiced their attack at a training station in Scotland. The real SOE attack, Operation Gunnerside in 1943, damaged the plant considerably, but the Germans rebuilt it. The American air force then bombed it. After that attack, Hitler ordered the operation to be moved to Germany.

MI-6 was not too worried about that plan, knowing that Germany was short of hydroelectric power. The problem was to prevent the Germans from moving the Vemork plant's store of heavy water to Germany. SOE learned that one leg of the trip would be by ferry across a lake. Knut Haukelid, one of the Norwegians in the Gunnerside attack, boldly went aboard the ferry with two other men. They planted an explosive in the bow, timing fuses to set the explosion off when the vessel was in deep water, and then went ashore. The next morning, right on schedule, the explosive went off and the ferry sank, carrying the heavy water to the bottom of the deep lake. Without heavy water, Germany's atomic research faltered, and the Germans never managed to develop an atomic bomb.

Two devastating weapons they did develop were the V-1 pilotless aircraft and the V-2 rocket. (The *V* came from *vergeltung*, the German word for vengeance.) Although most of the work was done on the Baltic island of Peenemünde

Hitler put a great deal of effort into developing the V-1 flying bomb and the V-2 rocket at Peenemünde. Allied espionage kept track of the work and Allied bombers put the program severely off track with a bombing attack in August 1943. Hitler was still able to launch a number of the weapons before surrendering in 1945. Here a V-1 was photographed over England in April 1944 from an American fighter plane that was about to fly alongside and flip it with a wingtip, causing it to crash in an open field. (Library of Congress)

that was mentioned in the Oslo Report, MI-6 for a long time suspected the German talk of V weapons as bluster.

Jones took the talk seriously and accumulated a good deal of information on the installation at Peenemünde and the nature of the weapons. He had help from what he viewed as one of the most remarkable spy reports of the war. It came from Amniarix (Jeannie Rousseau), a member of the large French network known as Alliance and also as Noah's Ark because the members referred to one another by the names of animals. Through friendship with a German officer, she had landed a job with the German regiment responsible for launching the V-1 toward London. Her report provided solid details about the V-weapon program.

Then, in 1943, another German report came to the hands of the MI-6 chief in Lisbon. (Menzies and others in MI-6 believed the hand of Canaris lay behind this report, the Oslo Report and other useful documents that reached the Allies from time to time.) The Lisbon Report, as it came to be known, described the work on V weapons and said: "Hitler and members of his Cabinet recently inspected both weapons at Peenemünde. About 10th June, Hitler told assembled military leaders that the Germans had only to hold out, since by the end of 1943 London would be leveled to the ground and Britain forced to capitulate . . . Production of both weapons is to have first priority."

The Allied response was Operation Hydra, a massive attack by RAF bombers on the Peenemünde installation during the night of August 17–18, 1943. It crippled the V-weapon program. Although Hitler moved production to an underground plant in the Harz Mountains and began attacking London with V-1's in June, 1944, and V-2's in September, he could not keep the attacks up for long because Allied troops soon overran the launching sites.

Meanwhile, the XX Committee helped to blunt the effect of the V weapons by having several of its double agents report to Germany that the weapons were landing beyond London. In fact, they were at first well aimed at central

A German V-2 is prepared for launching. The V-2s were much bigger than the V-1s and had a longer range. Allied double agents blunted the effects of the V weapons by reporting to the Germans that they were landing beyond London. In fact they were well aimed at central London, but because of the reports from the double agents the Germans shortened the range, causing the weapons to fall short of the nerve centers of the British government and the Allied command. (National Archives)

London, but the XX reports caused the Germans to shorten the range so that most of the missiles missed the nerve centers of the government.

The Jones group was also responsible for Moonshine. The RAF was eager to lure German fighter planes to take to the air any time British planes appeared over Germany, instead of responding only when the British attack appeared to be massive. The British were confident that they could down significant numbers of German fighter planes and so further weaken the Luftwaffe. Jones's response was to develop a receiving device that British planes could carry to pick up pulses from German radar and, as he put it, send back "longer, beating echoes to make it look as though a whole formation of aircraft were present." This was Moonshine. It turned out to be a success on airplanes, and in the preparation for the invasion of France the British used it on ships. The game was to make the Germans think a sizable fleet—instead of a few small launches—was bearing down on a region of the coast away from the scene of the actual invasion in Normandy.

***

The XX Committee had a pair of tricky tasks throughout the war. One was to play tricks on the Germans through the information passed to them by the double agents. The other was to avoid inadvertently passing information that was really valuable. It was in pursuit of this second goal that the committee took such great pains to make sure that information from one agent did not contradict what reached the Germans from another. The committee also took pains to avoid doing something that might give away the whole double-agent game.

John Masterman, writing about the work of the committee after the war, cited several benefits that the system brought to the British. The main one was control of the German espionage apparatus in Britain. "For the greater part of the war," he wrote, "we did much more than practise a large-scale deception through double agents; by means of the double-agent system *we actively ran and controlled the German espionage system in this country.*" In addition, the system provided the British with information about the people in the German espionage organization and the organization's methods of operation. A further benefit was that the information the Germans sought from the people they thought were their agents in England gave the British evidence of the enemy's intentions. Sometimes this knowledge enabled the British to influence the enemy's decisions; if the double agents told the Germans that British airports were poorly defended, the Germans might bomb airports instead of factories.

According to Masterman, the files of MI-5 held records of about 120 double agents. Some of the agents did not do much, or their operation fizzled. Masterman listed 39 agents—from BALLOON to ZIGZAG—who did "interesting" double-cross work under control from England. Among them were TRICYCLE, TATE and GARBO.

TRICYCLE was Dusko Popov, a Yugoslavian businessman recruited for the Abwehr by the German embassy in Belgrade and sent to England. There he got in touch with British authorities and became a double agent. Because he had good connections in Lisbon, another city harboring many spies from both sides in the war, the XX Committee often sent him there. One of his feats in Lisbon was Plan Midas.

Under the plan, TRICYCLE told his German contact that he knew a rich man in England who wanted to build up a supply of dollars in the United States against the possibility that England might lose the war. The Germans agreed to give TRICYCLE a large sum in dollars if the rich man would pay the equivalent in pounds to a German agent in London. The agent was TATE. The Germans, of course, did not know that both TRICYCLE and TATE were working for the XX Committee; indeed, they did not know the XX Committee existed.

As Masterman put it, "The value of the operation to us was considerable." TRICYCLE and TATE had performed what seemed to the Germans to be a useful service, so their value went up in German eyes. Moreover, the Germans thought they had put TATE in control of a goodly amount of money (20,000 pounds) that he could use in their interest in England. The real result, Masterman said, was that "we secured a considerable sum of money and were confirmed in our belief that we controlled the effective part of the German organisation in this country."

TATE was Wulf Schmidt, a German spy who parachuted into England in 1940. MI-5 quickly picked him up and convinced him to become a double agent. He established the record for durability, carrying on radio traffic with the Abwehr office in Hamburg from 1940 until a few hours before the Allies captured the city in 1945.

One of his triumphs was a naval deception worked out by Ewen Montagu. Late in the war, German U-boats gained an advantage through the development of the snorkel. Whereas previously every U-boat had to come to the surface regularly to take on fresh air, it could now merely stick the snorkel tube up while remaining below the surface, hard to detect. The only good counterstroke was to lay minefields, but the British were short of both mines and ships to lay them.

TATE was therefore given an imaginary friend said to be serving on a minelayer. Visiting TATE in London, the friend boasted of a new minefield being laid south of Ireland. (The minefield was as imaginary as the friend.) TATE reported this to the Germans and later told them that the minefield was in place. At about the same time, a U-boat in that area hit a mine—apparently one that had broken away from a distant spot—and sank. That was enough for the Germans. They closed the entire area of some 3,600 square miles to U-boats. It was an area passed through by many of the ships bringing supplies to the Allied forces that had invaded France, and the U-boats could have had good hunting there.

GARBO in effect invented himself. He offered his services to the Germans in 1941 with the intention of going over to the British as a double agent. The Germans took him on and sent him, they thought, to England, fitting him out with invisible ink, a cover story and a set of answers to questions he would be asked once he got there.

GARBO set out from Madrid but actually went no farther than Portugal. There, working with such modest tools as a printed guide to the British Isles, a timetable for English trains and a map of England, he composed a series of reports to the Abwehr. He also reported that he had recruited three subagents in England.

It was all fiction. As Masterman wrote of GARBO's months in Portugal, however, "Fiction suitably presented is often more easily credible than truth, and it was not long before the Germans came to trust his reports and to appreciate them highly." That situation soon posed a problem for the British. Some of GARBO's made-up reports were worrisomely close to the truth. Then the British learned through other sources that the Germans were preparing to attack a convoy supposedly on its way to the Mediterranean from Liverpool. On further investigation, they found that the convoy was one of GARBO's inventions. If the Germans put that much faith in his reports, it would be better to get him to England and put him to work as a genuine double agent. Moreover, GARBO was not very familiar with British ways. If the XX Committee did not soon take control of his operations, he might give himself away through some mistake, and the British would never get him. And so in the spring of 1942 they smuggled him into England.

There GARBO entered vigorously into the spirit of things. By the summer of 1944, he had built up a network of 14 active agents and 11 valuable contacts in such places as the Ministry of Information. They were all imaginary, dreamed up and given personalities by GARBO and Thomas Harris, his case officer in MI-5. Their pay from the Germans amounted to some 20,000 pounds, which went into British coffers. By

August, 1944, this fictional organization had supplied the Germans with some 400 secret letters and 2,000 long radio messages.

The activities of MUTT and JEFF also stand out. They were Norwegians carried to England in 1941 by a German seaplane and then put ashore by boat. They promptly turned themselves in, revealing that the Germans had provided them with a radio, a sum of money, forged ration books that were out of date, detonators and bicycles. The mission the Germans had given them was to sabotage installations in Scotland.

Orders from the Germans for their spies to commit sabotage presented the XX Committee with a hard problem. If no sabotage was done, the Germans might become suspicious of the agent. Yet real sabotage, such as blowing up an ammunition dump, would interfere with the war effort and pose danger to British soldiers and civilians. The XX Committee therefore let some of the agents carry out what could be called controlled sabotage. It didn't do a great deal of harm, but it built up the reputations of the agents in the eyes of the Germans, showed what kinds of sabotage equipment the Germans had developed and sometimes revealed what other sabotage operations the Germans had in mind.

The first such episode was plan Guy Fawkes in 1941. It called for a minor explosion in an area storing food. As Masterman wrote later, there were "many ticklish moments" before the operation succeeded. Two elderly people set to guard against fire were asleep, and it was difficult to rouse them and lure them away from the place where the explosion was being set. A local policeman almost arrested the people sent to set off the explosion. Finally, it was difficult to make sure that the fire caused by the explosion was strong enough to get notice in the newspapers, which would convince the Germans that the sabotage had succeeded, without causing serious damage before the firemen could put it out.

In 1942, under Plan Brock, MUTT and JEFF staged a blowup of some huts at a military installation. Again several things went wrong, requiring the authorities to plant additional clues before the deed was declared to be German sabotage and the newspapers took note of it.

A year later MUTT and JEFF carried out Plan Bunbury, which was a staged explosion at a generating station. The Germans agreed to supply money and equipment but dropped them in the wrong place, so that they had to make another delivery. The staged sabotage was a success. It built up in German eyes the reputation of two agents who were useful to the British; it also provided the British with samples of German equipment for sabotage and with information about German sabotage techniques.

Double agent BRONX, the daughter of a South American diplomat, supplied the Germans with misinformation by letter from London. In the period before the invasion of France, the Germans were concerned that information by letter would not reach them soon enough. So they arranged a code whereby BRONX would send a telegram to German agents in Lisbon asking for money that she needed for her dentist. The amount of money asked for would indicate where the invasion would come. The British saw to it that her information helped to throw the Germans off the scent.

Shortly after the war in Europe had ended and the double-cross operation was over, Masterman set out in a report "certain principles" the XX Committee had arrived at in the handling of double agents. (In 1972, he published the report, largely unchanged, as a book: *The Double-Cross System in the War of 1939 to 1945.*) One principle is that a double agent should "actually live the life and go through all the motions of a genuine agent." The experience will give his reports a true ring; and when, as often happened, he meets with his German controllers in a neutral country, he cannot easily be tripped up by trick questions. An extension of this idea is that the double agent should tell the enemy the truth as often as possible, because "a lie when it is needed will only be believed if it rests on a firm foundation of previous truth."

Another principle is that a double agent should always have a case officer who keeps closely in touch with what the agent does. Only in this way can the controlling organization make sure that what one agent does fits in with what the other agents are doing. "The most profitable cases," Masterman wrote, "were those in which the case officer had introduced himself most completely into the skin of the agent." One reason is that only a thorough record of each case can save the operation from making some blunder relating to an agent or the agent from giving himself away through some inconsistency.

It is best, the committee concluded, for a double agent to be paid. "The agent who is not treated generously," Masterman said, "is apt to become disgruntled, especially when he observes large sums coming to us through his instrumentality."

***

Ewen Montagu was involved in several deceptions besides Operation Mincemeat, and some of them drew on the services of double agents. One such case began when the Germans learned from careless talk by British merchant seamen that the British had a new antisubmarine weapon called Hedgehog. The Abwehr asked some of its supposed agents in England (who were actually double agents) for more information. Montagu worked out a plan whereby the double agents told the Germans the bare facts about the weapon—that it fired depth charges forward instead of dropping them astern (the usual practice)—and then embellished the facts. One embellishment was to let on the Hedgehog had a proximity fuse, so that the charge would go off if it got near a submarine. (Ordinary depth charges relied on a depth setting that in effect timed the explosion.) Another embellishment was to overstate the range and power of the weapon.

TATE helped in a deception aimed at discouraging the Germans from using a tactic they had developed to thwart

Asdic, an underwater submarine detector. The German tactic was to blow air out of a torpedo tube on a submarine, creating a mass of bubbles in the water. Asdic would focus on the bubbles, giving the submarine a chance to slip away.

The British knew of a U-boat that had been sunk in spite of blowing bubbles. TATE used this incident to give the Abwehr a made-up tale. He said he had entertained the commander of a British ship that had sunk a bubble-blowing submarine. The Germans, the commander reported, never knew "they were *helping* us" with the bubble tactic, because Asdic could detect reflections of the U-boat bouncing off the bubbles and thus could learn which way the submarine had gone in its effort to escape.

***

Several of the XX Committee's agents had roles in the major deception of the war, Plan Bodyguard. The name came from a remark by Churchill in 1943 at the conference of the Allied leaders—Roosevelt, Churchill and Josef Stalin—in Teheran. "In wartime," Churchill said, "truth is so precious that she should always be attended by a bodyguard of lies."

The truth that was to be protected by a bodyguard of lies was that the Allied invasion of Europe would take place in Normandy. The deceptions, orchestrated by the London Controlling Section, sought to build in Hitler's mind the belief that attacks might come in a number of other places. One part of the plan was Fortitude North, which sought to make Hitler keep substantial forces in Norway in the belief that the Allies might mount an attack there. Fortitude South sought to convince him that the landing place in France would be the Pas de Calais—the area closest to England. A possible attack in Greece went by the name of Operation Zeppelin and one in southern France was Operation Vendetta.

Fortitude South was the most elaborate scheme. Its main element was a phony force, FUSAG (First United States

A dummy airplane is inflated by Allied soldiers as part of Operation Bodyguard, a deception designed to persuade the Germans that the Allies were building up a force north of London for an invasion of France at Pas de Calais. The "force" was largely imaginary, but the deception made the Germans believe in it and keep many of their defenses away from the Normandy coast where the invasion actually took place in June 1944. (U.S. Army Intelligence and Security Command)

Army Group), apparently preparing to attack the Pas de Calais from England. It was a force largely made up of dummy tanks, guns and vehicles. Intense radio traffic went on among its "units." Double agents sent in a flow of reports of activity by FUSAG components.

The success of all this deception was reflected in a German war map captured in Italy three weeks before the landing in Normandy. It showed the arrangement of Allied forces as the Germans understood the situation, and there they were—all the phony units, located and identified almost entirely according to the misinformation supplied through Fortitude South.

The deception continued even after the landing in Normandy. Within a few days of the landing, German generals were urging Hitler to shift units there from the Pas de Calais. GARBO went to work again. "The present assault," he said in a message to Berlin, "is a trap set with the purpose of making us move all our reserves in a rushed strategic redisposition which we would later regret." The attack on Normandy was only a diversion, he said; the real attack would come soon in the Pas de Calais.

Hitler issued an order. The troops in the Pas de Calais were to stay there, and reinforcements were to be sent in. Sir Ronald Wingate, deputy chief of LCS, told of Churchill's reaction when word of Hitler's order arrived: "The P.M. [prime minister] came in with Stewart Menzies and the P.M. said this was the crowning achievement of the long and glorious history of the British Secret Service."

6

ULTRA
Britain Breaks the German Codes

The telephone rings at Chequers, the official country home of Britain's prime minister. Winston Churchill's private secretary answers. As soon as he hears the caller is Group Captain F. W. Winterbotham, he knows Churchill will want to come to the phone. Winterbotham is the chief protector of Ultra, which Churchill calls "my most secret source," and he telephones only when he has another gem from that source. The private secretary asks Winterbotham to hold the line.

"There would be a pause," Winterbotham wrote later, "until I heard heavy breathing at the other end and I knew it was time to identify myself by name and begin to read . . . Sometimes, as the war progressed, there would be long political despatches from Hitler to his governors in his new empire; these intrigued Churchill, and I would be asked to read them all over again to some other Cabinet minister who was spending the weekend at Chequers. At other times there would just be a 'thank you,' but always one had to wait for it because sometimes the Prime Minister would mull the signal over in his mind and then come back with an order to take some action with the Ministry concerned. That well-known voice was always courteous."

The Enigma machine was the coding device the Germans believed to be impenetrable because it gave the operator so many ways of changing the code. The British cryptanalysts at Bletchley Park built the "Bombe," a machine that could decode the Enigma messages. As a result of this "most secret source," called Ultra, the Allies had a window into the German camp throughout most of the war. (National Archives)

The key to the achievements of Ultra was the success of the British at solving the intricacies of Enigma, the coding machine in which the Germans put unshakeable faith. The first version of the machine was invented in 1919 by a Dutchman, Hugo Koch. He did not get far with the idea and soon turned the rights over to a German engineer,

Artur Scherbius, who built a machine that he saw mainly as a tool for businessmen. "The natural inquisitiveness of competitors," he said in a brochure on his device, "is at once checkmated by a machine which enables you to keep all your documents . . . entirely secret."

Scherbius's machine and the later versions looked something like the typewriters of the day. Enigma had a typewriter keyboard on which the operator wrote his message in ordinary German. Above the keyboard the message appeared on a lighted panel in entirely different letters. What happened was that the machine's intricate innards of rotors and electrical circuits changed each letter each time the operator struck that letter on the keyboard. The letter *G*, for example, might show up on the panel as *L* one time and *E* the next. The coded message went out by radio or telephone. The operator at the receiving end set his machine according to the prearranged daily or hourly key and typed the message he had received. The machine would put up on the lighted panel the original message in plain German. Enigma gave the operator wide scope for resetting its controls, and so the machine had an enormous capacity for generating codes.

By 1934, the German government had taken an interest in Enigma, and the coding machine soon became exclusively theirs. During the course of the war, they made something like 100,000 of the machines and distributed them widely in the government and the military services.

The British were naturally interested in the new German coding system, and MI-6 set out to learn what lay behind it. In June of 1938, they had a stroke of luck. An MI-6 agent had met a Polish engineer who had worked at the factory in Berlin that built the machines. The Pole offered to sell the British the secrets of the machine and to build a duplicate.

Menzies was keenly interested, but he wanted to be sure the Pole was not a German plant intended to lead the British down a false trail. He sent two experts in cryptography—Alfred Dilwyn Knox and Alan Turing—to Warsaw to see the man. They were impressed, and Menzies accepted the deal. The British moved the Pole to Paris, and there he built a machine that showed MI-6 what the Germans had done to improve Enigma.

Later, in one of the most memorable episodes of the war, the British got the real thing. In May 1941, the German submarine U-110 attacked a convoy near Greenland. A counterattack by the British destroyer *Bulldog* forced the sub to the surface, where the crew abandoned it. They left explosives timed to destroy it, but the explosives failed to go off. Five sailors from *Bulldog* rowed through heavy seas to put a boarding party on the sub. The commander of the party, Sub-Lieutenant David Balme of the Royal Navy, made his way through the silent and darkened sub to the communications room. There he found an intact Enigma and the code books that went with it. In a long and perilous operation, Balme and his crew got these vital prizes out of the sub and back to *Bulldog*.

But having a machine was not enough. The British still had to figure out how to recognize quickly when the settings of a German Enigma had been changed and what the new settings were. Their answer, to which Turing made major contributions, was the "Bombe," the first of several machines that worked by matching the electrical circuits of Enigma. (To this day, the British have kept secret the details of how the Bombe worked. H. M. Keen, the chief engineer of the project, said in an interview with the author Anthony Cave Brown that "its secret was in the internal wiring of [Enigma's] rotors, which The Bombe sought to imitate." Another person familiar with the machine has said that what it did was "to test all the possible wheel or rotor orders of the Enigma, all the possible wheel settings and plug . . . connections to discover which of the possible arrangements would match a prescribed combination of letters.") The Bombe provided the path to the pivotal achievement of cracking the German codes.

With that achievement, the small British cryptanalysis operation—the Government Code and Cypher School— soon turned into a major enterprise. In its new headquarters at Bletchley Park, it grew from 90 people at the start of the war to 9,000 at the peak of the fighting.

Long afterward, Winterbotham remembered the Bombe's first breakthrough in 1940. "It was just as the bitter cold days of that frozen winter were giving way to the first days of April sunshine that the oracle of Bletchley spoke and Menzies handed me four little slips of paper, each with a short Luftwaffe message dealing with personnel postings to units. From the Intelligence point of view they were of little value . . . but to the backroom boys at Bletchley Park and to Menzies, and indeed to me, they were like the magic in the pot of gold at the end of the rainbow. The miracle had arrived."

Miracles came profusely from Bletchley after that day. Ultra listened in as the Germans made their preparations for Sealion, their plan to invade England. Through Ultra, the British learned about Eagle Day—September 15, 1940, when the Germans planned a massive attack by the Luftwaffe to knock out the Royal Air Force as a prelude to the invasion. Knowing the plan in detail, the British were able to focus the slender resources of the RAF and their antiaircraft defenses on the most strategically important spots, and they beat off the attack.

The juiciest plum came two days later. Ultra revealed an order from Hitler to dismantle the equipment that had been set up at Dutch airfields to load airplanes with paratroopers and equipment. It meant he was postponing the invasion. A few months later, the Ultra traffic began to reveal that Hitler was moving his forces eastward, away from the invasion area, in preparation for an attack on Russia. That meant the end of Sealion.

Another miracle at Bletchley in 1940 was the cracking of the Abwehr code. Ultra could now listen in on what the German spy apparatus was doing and planning. With that leverage, the British were on the way to the kind of manipulation of Abwehr done by the XX Committee.

With Ultra producing a flow of German secrets totally beyond what could be expected from normal espionage, it was obvious that the Allies would have to impose tough controls on the use of this "Special Intelligence" to make sure the Germans remained unaware that their codes had been penetrated. To that end, the British laid down some regulations on the subject: "The extreme importance of Special Intelligence as a source of reliable information concerning enemy activities and intentions has been repeatedly proved. Preservation of this source requires that the enemy be given no reason to suspect that his communications are being read . . . . Extreme secrecy is therefore required."

Churchill put Winterbotham in charge of carrying out the regulations, and Winterbotham set himself three goals. The first was, as he put it, "absolute ruthlessness in keeping to a minimum the number of people who were allowed to receive and be aware of Ultra." The second was to make sure that no Ultra documents reached the battlefield, where they might fall into German hands. To this end, MI-6 set up Special Liaison Units, known as SLUs, that were attached to each major headquarters in the field. The men in these units gave Ultra secrets orally to the commanders authorized to receive them. The SLUs also reminded the commanders constantly of Winterbotham's third goal, which was to make certain that any action they took on the basis of information from Ultra was made to look as though it arose from some other source—information from spies, prisoners of war or captured documents; reconnaissance flights over an area before an attack; leaks from neutral diplomats or anti-Nazi Germans; perhaps even a betrayal by Germany's Italian allies, whom the Germans mistrusted anyway.

The regulations worked, and the miracles continued. One of them was a major contribution to the British navy's victory over the Italian fleet in the eastern Mediterranean. In

March 1941, Ultra's eavesdropping on the radio traffic of the Luftwaffe and the Italian navy picked up their plans for an attack on British ship convoys in the Mediterranean. The date set was March 27. Making an aerial reconnaissance over the Italian fleet to disguise the source of the foreknowledge, the British fleet based in Egypt steamed out to meet and overpower the Italian ships.

It is possible that the effort to protect Ultra was sometimes costly. Some observers have thought the bombing of Coventry was such a case.

Ultra had picked up in November 1940 the German plan for a bombing attack under the name of Moonlight Sonata. It was to be Hitler's revenge for an attack the RAF had made on Munich during the evening of November 8, when Hitler was scheduled to speak there in commemoration of the 17th anniversary of the Beer Hall Putsch of 1923—his first attempt to gain power.

According to Ultra, the Moonlight Sonata attack was to be made on the night of November 14 against three cities identified by code names, among them *Korn*. This information was known by November 11. People close to Churchill have said the government did not know, however, that *Korn* was Coventry. Others have maintained that there were at least hints of an attack on Coventry. The argument is that the Churchill government had time to take defensive measures or warn the people of Coventry but that Churchill refused to do so because of the danger of revealing the Ultra secret. The facts of what Churchill was doing that evening suggest that he was expecting an attack on London. Whatever the truth of the matter, Coventry took a fearful pounding.

Even in defeat, Ultra made a valuable contribution. It let the British learn in detail the German plans for invading Crete in 1941. Although the British built up their defenses, they were still short of men and ships, and the island fell. But the Germans took such heavy casualties among their paratroopers that Hitler was never able to mount another major airborne attack.

In May 1941, the boost to Ultra from the U-110 incident and the confiscated Enigma machine helped the British track the course of the German battleship *Bismarck* after her escape from an attack by the British battleship *Prince of Wales* and three cruisers. British ships, together with torpedo planes from the carrier *Ark Royal*, attacked the *Bismarck* and sank her. The German had intended to use their powerful battleship as the mainstay of their attack on Allied shipping in the Atlantic.

The *Bismarck* affair and other disasters of the period raised in the minds of the Germans the possibility that the British were reading the Enigma code. The authorities in Berlin set up a board of inquiry to look into the possibility. This board came to the same conclusion reached by all the other German groups that considered the matter during the war. "It is not necessary," the board said, "to put the blame on a breach of security as regards the code and cipher tables." Who was to blame? Well, the board thought, MI-6 was probably tapping the German telephone lines that ran through occupied territory. Or the MI-6 spy network, which the Germans viewed as highly efficient, had scored again. Or anti-Nazi Germans had tipped off the British.

This attitude probably contributed as much to the success of Ultra as the Allied effort at protection did. Several times during the war there were scares about the safety of Ultra, usually because some commander could not wait to disguise the source of his information before pouncing on the Germans. But the Germans were absolutely convinced that the codes generated by Enigma could not be broken.

Meanwhile, the people at Bletchley Park continued to break the Enigma codes. In 1942, they solved the German weather code. Thereafter, the Allies knew what the Germans knew about the weather over Britain and Allied battle positions and could launch attacks at times when the Germans thought the weather was unfavorable for an attack. Being able to read the weather code was also a great boon for the Allies when they began their massive bombing raids on Germany, because the pilots could be briefed accurately on the weather they would encounter. Winterbotham sat in on some of the briefings. He later wrote: "I would watch the care with which the meteorological officer would outline the weather all the way to the target and back. No one, I am glad to say, asked him how he knew it, but if someone queried the forecast, 'Tooey' Spaatz [Major General Carl Spaatz, the American who commanded the strategic bombing forces operating from England] would look across at me with a twinkle in those shrewd eyes behind his gold-rimmed glasses and say quietly, 'I think you can rely on that.'"

In the largely British battle with Axis (German and Italian) forces in North Africa before Operation Torch, Ultra supplied the British commanders with precise information on what forces the enemy had and when and where they would attack. Ultra had another role, which was to keep the British fleet alerted to the movement of convoys from Italy that sought to supply the Axis forces in North Africa. A convoy would set out. Ultra would alert the British. They would send a reconnaissance plane over the convoy to cover up the real reason for knowing where the convoy was. Then British naval vessels would close in and sink the convoy.

Once it was foggy, and the British were unable to send a reconnaissance plane over a convoy that had set out from Naples. Nevertheless, they showed up at the right place and time to send the convoy to the bottom. The German commanders were suspicious about this episode and sent a message to the Abwehr asking how the British could have known where and when to attack in a fog. Ultra revealed the message. Winterbotham responded by sending a telegram addressed to a nonexistent British spy in Naples. He put it in a code he knew the Germans could read. The message thanked the spy for information about the convoy and told him his pay would be raised.

The result of the flow of information from Ultra was a massive British victory in North Africa. Because of Ultra, the Axis forces were outmaneuvered on the battlefield and starved for supplies. As the official British history of the war said later, "British forces in North Africa were supplied with more information about more aspects of the enemy's operations than any forces enjoyed during any important campaign in the Second World War."

By 1943, Ultra was picking up for the Allies as many as 4,000 secret German communications a day. Together they presented a detailed picture of how Hitler planned to meet the oncoming invasion of Europe (Operation Neptune) and what forces he had for it.

An Allied convoy steams toward England with supplies in 1942. At the time, German submarines were wreaking havoc on such convoys, but Ultra's penetration of the German naval codes helped to turn aside the U-boat attacks by the summer of 1943. (National Archives)

A symbol of the turn of the tide in the U-boat war is this attack in June 1943 on the German submarine U-118. Planes from the U.S.S. Pogue *are dropping depth charges, one of which is exploding close to the sub.* (National Archives)

At the same time, it was largely because of Ultra that Hitler failed in an effort to win the war without having to repel the invasion in land battles. That effort was his powerful and prolonged U-boat attack on the ship convoys that carried supplies to England, including the supplies and troops that would make Neptune possible. The toll was devastating: 4.3 million tons of shipping in 1941, 7.8 million in 1942. Grand Admiral Karl Doenitz, commander of the U-boat fleet, believed Germany could win the war if the U-boats sank 800,000 tons of shipping per month. The U-boats came close to that in November 1942.

In all of this they were aided by the fact that the German command put a new cipher into effect for the U-boats early in 1942. In was called Triton, and for some time it eluded the codebreakers at Bletchley Park. It took them until December to break the Triton code.

By the beginning of 1943, the Germans had more than 100 U-boats in the North Atlantic. They were organized into "wolfpacks"—groups of submarines that operated together—strung across the Atlantic on the convoy route. It appeared possible that Doenitz would achieve Hitler's goal of strangling the Allies through U-boat assaults on Allied shipping.

By May, however, the tide had begun to turn. The Allies were at last able to commit to the battle better weapons for attacking the U-boats. They also had Ultra again after the interlude of darkness caused by Triton. Ultra told them where the wolfpacks were and where they planned to attack next. With this information, a convoy could be steered away from the danger area while Allied planes and ships hastened there to attack the wolfpacks. As Peter Calvocoressi, who worked at Bletchley Park, put it later, "Ultra enabled the Admiralty to play hide and seek in the Atlantic with its eyes open."

The Germans tried to improve their scores by sending out "milchcows," which were supply ships that met U-boats at sea and resupplied them with fuel and other necessities. The aim was to keep the U-boats at sea for a longer time before they had to return to port. Ultra kept the Allies posted on where the milchcows were, and Allied forces sank them one by one. Winterbotham thought this "must have been one of the greatest blows suffered by the U-boats."

By the summer of 1943, it was clear that the Germans had lost the battle of the North Atlantic. The U-boats were no longer knocking out Allied shipping at a paralyzing rate, whereas the Allies were taking a fearsome toll of the U-boats.

In this losing battle as in others, the Germans wondered how the Allies could be so devastatingly accurate in finding U-boats and milchcows. Several times they set up boards of inquiry to find out if the enemy was reading the Enigma codes, and each time they concluded that Enigma was impenetrable.

After the war, Doenitz discussed this problem in his memoirs. As a result of the turn of the tide in the battle of the

North Atlantic, he said, "we naturally went once more very closely into the question of what knowledge the enemy could possibly have of our U-boat dispositions . . . That a widespread spy network was at work in our bases in occupied France was something we obviously had to assume . . . Our ciphers were checked and rechecked, to make sure that they were unbreakable, and on each occasion the head of the Naval Intelligence Service at Naval High Command adhered to his opinion that it would be impossible for the enemy to decipher them. And to this day [1958], as far as I know, we are not certain whether or not the enemy did succeed in breaking our ciphers during the war. "

In the 11 months that the Allies battled Hitler on the ground in Europe, from June 1944 until the German surrender the following May, Ultra kept up a steady flow of what the German commanders were doing. "With this 'new dimension of war,'" Winterbotham wrote, "not only the commanders in the field, but also Churchill, Roosevelt and the Allied chiefs of staff had all the cards in the pack spread out on the table face upwards." Churchill said simply: "It was thanks to Ultra that we won the war."

7

MAGIC
America Breaks the Japanese Codes

In 1944, Governor Thomas E. Dewey of New York was the Republican nominee for President, campaigning against President Roosevelt's bid for a fourth term. Reports reaching Washington said Dewey intended to reveal that the United States had been able to break some Japanese codes before the war. Dewey would claim, the reports said, that with knowledge of the codes the Roosevelt Administration should have prevented the attack on Pearl Harbor or at least ought to have been better prepared for it.

The reports put General George C. Marshall, the Army Chief of Staff, in a tight spot. He thought it was absolutely vital to the war effort to prevent the Japanese from learning that the Americans were reading their codes. Yet if he tried to urge Dewey not to talk about code-breaking, he would be open to the charge that as an official of the Administration he was trying to give Roosevelt an edge in the campaign.

Marshall wrote Dewey a letter and had it delivered personally by Colonel Carter Clarke, who was in charge of the most secret documents of the War and Navy departments. Emphasizing that he was acting on his own and that the President did not know of the letter, Marshall said:

> The most vital evidence in the Pearl Harbor matter consists of our intercepts of the Japanese diplomatic communications. Over a period of years our cryptograph people analyzed the character of the machine the Japanese were using for encoding their diplomatic messages. Based on this a corresponding machine was built by us

General George C. Marshall, U.S. Army Chief of Staff in World War II, persuaded the Republican candidate for president in 1944—Governor Thomas E. Dewey of New York—not to reveal that the Allies had broken the German and Japanese codes. Marshall's letter to Dewey was part of an intensive Allied effort to protect Ultra and Magic. Those code-breaking operations remained unknown to the Germans and Japanese until long after the war. (National Archives)

which deciphers their messages. Therefore, we possessed a wealth of information regarding their moves in the Pacific . . . but which unfortunately made no reference whatever to intentions toward Hawaii until the last message before December 7th (the day of the Japanese attack), which did not reach our hands until the following day, December 8th.

Now the point to the present dilemma is that we have gone ahead with this business of deciphering their codes until we possess other codes, German as well as Japanese . . . You will understand from the foregoing the utterly tragic consequences if the present political debates regarding Pearl Harbor disclose to the enemy, German or Jap, any suspicion of the vital sources of information we possess.

Dewey took the point. He did not say anything in his campaign about code-breaking. Nor did he let slip any of the information Marshall included in his letter about what the Allies had accomplished with knowledge of the enemy codes.

The main figure among the "cryptograph people" mentioned by Marshall was William F. Friedman, head of the U.S. Army's Signal Intelligence Service. By 1939, he had focused on the task of understanding the Japanese code machine that the Americans called Purple. (The Japanese called it the J machine, Alphabetical Typewriter, 97-*shiki*

This analogue of the Japanese Purple coding machine was built by William Friedman and his associates in the U.S. Signal Intelligence Service to decipher Japanese diplomatic messages in 1941. The SIS group built the machine without access to the workings of the real Purple machine. (U.S. Army Intelligence and Security Command)

William Friedman (center) and his small group of associates in the Signal Intelligence Service appear in this photograph from the 1930s. (U.S. Army Intelligence and Security Command)

O-bun In-ji-Ki, Type 97. The 97 came from the Japanese year 2597—our 1937, the year the machine went into operation.)

To say merely that Friedman succeeded is to mask the difficulty of the task, because the machine was as formidable at coding as the German Enigma was. In addition, the Japanese were working in a language far stranger to English-speaking people than German is. But succeed Friedman did, partly because of some old-fashioned spy work by American agents who, carrying hidden miniature cameras, managed to get into three Japanese embassies that had a Purple machine. The agents took pictures, which were enlarged to 10 times the size of the actual machine.

Pictures alone were not enough; like Alan Turing when he tackled the Enigma problem, Friedman had to fathom the inner workings of Purple and find a way of keeping up with the regular changes the Japanese made in the code. He had a bit more help, this time from the Japanese. Before Friedman broke the Purple code, he had broken the Japanese cipher that the Americans called the Red code. Even though the Japanese did not know that, they made a mistake that cryptographers should not make. Occasionally they sent a message in the Red code and the same message in the Purple code. Knowing the Red code, the American cryptanalysts could compare a deciphered Red message with an undeciphered Purple one and get a big boost in solving the Purple code.

One of Friedman's helpers, Frank Rowlett, said later that because of the success in breaking Purple, "the chief signal officer liked to refer to us as magicians." From that habit, the decoded Purple messages came to be known as Magic.

With this magical ability to listen in on the enemy's business, the American decoding operation quickly grew into a big enterprise. On the day the Japanese attacked Pearl Harbor and brought the Americans into the war, the Signal Intelligence Service had 181 people at work in Washington. When the war ended, there were 7,000, and SIS had long since taken over the entire campus of Arlington Hall, a girls' school in the Virginia suburbs of Washington. The navy had a similarly enlarged decoding enterprise working on Japanese naval signals.

Magic and Ultra teamed up early in the war to give the Japanese one of their first defeats. Germany, as Japan's ally, was trying to ship supplies to Japan in vessels called Yanagi transports. On the way out and on the way back, they had to run a blockade maintained by the British off the coast of France. Magic kept track of the traffic, largely through the messages sent to Tokyo by Ambassador Oshima in Berlin, and Ultra kept track of the signals from the German U-boats assigned to escort the transports through the blockade. The result was a steady sinking of the Yanagi transports and a slow choking off of the German supply line to Japan. After one such sinking in 1943, U-264 of the escort group signaled

Eventually the Signal Intelligence Service grew so large that it took over Arlington Hall in Virginia, formerly a girls' school. This building at Arlington Hall was headquarters for the American code-breaking operation known as Magic. (U.S. Army Intelligence and Security Command)

bleakly to U-boat headquarters that the "object-to-be-protected was sunk by a heavy cruiser, London class." So many objects-to-be-protected were sunk that in 1944 the Germans gave up the Yanagi operation.

It was American naval intelligence that contributed mightily to the navy's victory in the battle of Midway, which has often been called the turning point of the war against Japan because it showed that the Japanese were no longer able to dominate the Pacific. By June 1942, only six months after the disaster at Pearl Harbor, naval intelligence had broken the Japanese fleet code, known as JN25. Admiral Chester W. Nimitz, the American commander, had what amounted to a permanent wiretap on the plans of Admiral Isoroku Yamamoto, the Japanese commander. It soon became apparent, partly because of an American ruse, that Yamamoto was planning an attack at Midway.

That ruse was the idea of Jasper Holmes, an American naval intelligence officer. The Japanese had been referring to the Midway plan by the code letters AF, and the Americans were not sure at first that the code meant Midway. Holmes proposed secretly telling the American command at Midway to send out an uncoded radio message that their plant for distilling fresh water had broken down. Sure enough, Japanese naval intelligence in Tokyo soon broadcast a message telling the attack force that AF had a shortage of fresh water.

The Japanese duly went ahead with their plans, and in early June of 1942, Yamamoto's fleet was bearing down on Midway. Nimitz, knowing of the plans, was ready. Among other things in the fierce battle on June 4, the Americans sank the Japanese aircraft carriers *Akaqi, Hiryu, Kaqa* and *Soryu*, which made up the heart of Yamamato's fleet.

Nimitz said after the battle that Midway "was essentially a victory of intelligence." An analysis of the battle by the American naval intelligence operation said: "Claims made ever since the last World War by Combat Intelligence experts in every nation of the world, as to the usefulness of cryptanalysis and the [radio] traffic analysis during the course of a sea battle, were proved beyond further doubt at Midway."

Traffic analysis proved its value on many occasions, particularly when for some reason the ability to penetrate enemy codes was temporarily blocked. An example was the campaign in the Solomon Islands in the southwest Pacific, which the Japanese occupied in 1942 and U.S. forces captured in 1943. An American assessment of the campaign said:

> Ten years before war broke out in the Pacific, American communication intelligence experts had foreseen that cryptanalysis would

be of little use during periods which immediately followed a major change in an enemy's cryptographic systems. Consequently a method had been devised which derived intelligence from various external characteristics of the enemy's communication system . . . This method, called traffic analysis, was not expected to be as accurate in its forecasts of enemy plans as cryptanalysis would be, but the experts hoped that it would have great potential value in time of war. These hopes were fully realized in the months of July and August 1942 . . . Traffic analysis was able to reveal the presence of the enemy in the Solomons, which occasioned the landing of the Marines there.

***

Less than a year after the Battle of Midway, Yamamoto himself fell victim to Magic. On April 14, 1943, American naval intelligence at Pearl Harbor picked up a coded Japanese message revealing that Yamamoto was going to make

A Japanese heavy cruiser has suffered heavy damage from carrier-based American naval aircraft at the Battle of Midway in June 1944. The American victory at Midway has been called the turning point of the war in the East because it showed that the Japanese could no longer dominate the Pacific. Thanks to Magic, the U.S. knew when and where to meet the attacking Japanese fleet. (Library of Congress)

an inspection trip in the Pacific on the 18th. The message gave details about the time he would arrive at and depart from each place. (On learning that this message had gone out, the commander of the Japanese Eleventh Air Flotilla said: "What a damned fool thing to do, to send such a long and detailed message about the activities of the C.-in-C. [commander-in-chief] so near the Front. This kind of thing must stop!")

Yamamoto's route was within range of American fighter planes. Clearly, it would be possible to intercept his flight and shoot him down. Nimitz, realizing that such a pinpoint attack on a small group of planes (Yamamoto's and six fighter escorts) in midair over the vast Pacific might make the Japanese suspicious that the Americans were reading their code, asked permission from Washington to go ahead. The problem went to the secretary of the navy, Frank Knox, and to President Roosevelt. They approved the attack, and on April 18, a flight of American P-38 fighters sent Yamamoto to his death.

This adventure did not go over well with Menzies. He thought the risk to Ultra and Magic was too great for the reward. What use was it to eliminate Yamamoto? He was a commander whose methods the Americans knew, and now he would be replaced by someone whose methods they did not know. But the trouble passed, and if the Japanese had suspicions about the security of their code, they at least did not switch to a different code. The rewards of Magic continued.

Among them was the rich lode of information about Hitler's plans contained in Ambassador Oshima's messages to Tokyo, which were picked up by Magic. As General Marshall said in his letter to Governor Dewey, "Our main basis of information regarding Hitler's intentions in Europe is obtained from Baron Oshima's messages from Berlin reporting his interviews with Hitler and other officials to the Japanese Government."

One highly useful set of reports from Oshima dealt with Germany's work on jet-propelled aircraft. Jet propulsion was new then, and the Germans were ahead of the Allies in developing it. Because the Japanese were keen to get into jet propulsion too, Oshima and his aides sent many reports on the subject. Magic revealed them all.

The Allied invasion of Europe also got a huge boost from Oshima and Magic. The ambassador was a good observer who traveled a lot, and his reports on Germany's defense arrangements were splendidly detailed. One of them was his report in December 1943 of his inspection of the Atlantic Wall. By the time of the invasion, the Allies knew such details as what troops they would be facing, where the German antiaircraft guns were and how the Germans had set up their antitank weapons and machine guns. To get anything like the same amount of information from spies on the ground would have been almost impossible, and the effort surely would have cost dearly in terms of spies who were killed, tortured or captured.

By 1943, the Americans had broken the Japanese military code. They were already reading the diplomatic and naval codes; now they could keep up with the activity of the Japanese army and its air force. It was a tough task, however, because the code was complicated and many of the reports concerned small movements by small units. The big picture had to be put together at Arlington Hall. As a government report put it after the war: "The high level Japanese military cryptographic systems were of such difficulty that only a tremendous organization equipped with expensive and bulky electrical tabulating machinery could produce any results. Consequently, detailed items of immediate tactical significance to an Army commander in the field could be read at Arlington Hall, but could not be produced by an agency located in the [combat] theater and near the Army commander interested. Therefore 'combat intelligence' was being produced in Washington, some 15,000 miles away from the front lines."

This kind of intelligence made many battles in the Pacific easier for the Americans and far less costly in lost men and equipment than they would have been otherwise. But Magic's greatest contribution to the defeat of the Japanese was probably in "the battle of the *marus*." *Maru* was the Japanese word for a merchant ship, which carried cargo, or a transport ship, which carried troops. Over the course of the war, American submarines sank so many *marus* that the Japanese economy, which depended on them for such crucial supplies as oil, was slowly strangled. The reason for the high score against *marus* was that Magic was supplying the American submarine command with the location of each *maru* every day it was at sea. "There were nights," Holmes said, "when nearly every American submarine on patrol in the central Pacific was working on the basis of information derived from cryptanalysis."

It was not easy at first. American torpedoes at the beginning of the war were notoriously inaccurate, tending to run too deep in the water. A submarine commander would line up a *maru* in his periscope and fire torpedoes that should have sunk it. But the torpedoes would miss, and the *maru* would continue on its way.

It took the naval authorities in Washington a long time to recognize the problem, but at last they developed torpedoes that found the target when a submarine commander had it in his sights. And he usually did have it in his sights because of Magic.

A score in June 1943, shows the power of Magic, although it involves a Japanese warship rather than a *maru*. (Bear in mind that as the war went on, the Americans tended to refer to all decoded material except the diplomatic messages as Ultra, following the British usage.) The American submarines *Salmon* and *Trigger* were on patrol in the Japanese Inland Sea when they received a message from ComSubPac (commander of submarines, Pacific):

"ANOTHER HOT ULTRA COMSUBPAC . . . LARGEST AND NEWEST NIP [JAPANESE] CARRIER WITH TWO DESTROYERS DEPARTS YOKOSUKA AT 5 HOURS GCT 10 JUNE AND CRUISES AT 22 KNOTS UNTIL REACHING

33–55 NORTH 140 EAST WHERE THEY REDUCE SPEED TO 18 KNOTS AND CHANGE COURSE TO 230 DEGREES. SALMON AND TRIGGER INTERCEPT IF POSSIBLE."

They did, hitting and badly damaging the carrier *Hiyo*. The result was another message from ComSubPac:

"COMSUBPAC SENDS ULTRA TO SALMON OR TRIGGER. CONGRATULATIONS TO WHICHEVER OF YOU DID THE BEAUTIFUL JOB. BOTH NOTE THAT ABOUT HALF THE NIP NAVY IS NOW ENGAGED IN TRYING TO TOW THE BIG FLAT TOP BACK TO YOKOSUKA."

That was the way things went for the Japanese after their initial successes. When the war was over, the Japanese issued a war history in many volumes. Chapter 14 of Volume 24 carried the title, "Examination of the Failure of Our Operations." It recognized, as the Japanese had failed to do throughout the war, that the Americans had broken the Japanese code. "Breaking our code," the history said, "undoubtedly increased the reliability of America's strategic estimates and furnished them with a substantial outline of our plans for the future."

CONCLUSION
The Effects of the Secret War

Not long after the battle of Cape Matapan in 1941—the naval encounter in which the British, with powerful aid from Ultra, put the Italian fleet out of commission—the Germans mounted Operation Mercury, an invasion of Crete. Hitler's aim was to push out the British air and naval forces operating from Crete and make the island a base for German operations in the eastern Mediterranean.

Once again Ultra provided the British with a clear advance look at the German plans and the strength of Hitler's forces. This time, however, that was not enough. Even though the British knew where the German airborne troops would land and where the German naval thrust would be, and even though they beefed up their own defenses at those places in anticipation of the attack, they simply did not have enough forces. They lost Crete.

The point of the story is that espionage alone will not win battles, even if it lets you know in advance almost everything about the enemy's plans. You have to have enough forces to withstand an attack or mount a successful offensive. The Allies would not have won the war without their superiority in manpower, weapons, planes, ships and manufacturing capacity. Without Ultra and Magic, however, they probably would not have won it as soon as they did, and the cost in lost and wounded men, downed airplanes, sunken ships and bombed cities surely would have been much greater.

Suppose the war had been fought without Ultra and Magic, as indeed most people thought it was until Winterbotham told the Ultra story in 1974. It would have been very hard to get many spies behind the German and

Japanese lines. The copious flow of information about German plans that Baron Oshima sent to Tokyo from Berlin would have been untapped. Battles like Midway might not have been fought because the American navy would not have had much information about where Yamamoto's fleet was or what its strength was. The invasion of Europe might have failed for want of information about the Atlantic Wall and other German defenses, and it would have been necessary to try again. The stranglehold that German U-boats fastened on Allied shipping in the North Atlantic would have been much harder to break. By the same token, the stranglehold of American submarines on Japanese shipping in the Pacific would have been far weaker.

It is also unlikely that the marvelous counterespionage operation guided by the XX Committee or the massive deceptions like Operation Bodyguard would have accomplished much, or perhaps even been possible, without Ultra. Those operations depended on Ultra for clues about the best ways to fool the Germans—as, for example, in leading them to believe the Allied invasion of Europe in 1944 would strike the Pas de Calais instead of Normandy.

Still, the Japanese and the Germans operated under some severe handicaps that would have hurt them even in a war fought without Ultra and Magic. The Japanese had to maintain forces spread out over an enormous part of the globe that mostly consisted of ocean. Putting spies in Allied fleets and divisions spread over the same area was virtually impossible.

The Germans had the *Schwarze Kapelle*, which did its best to thwart Hitler's ambitions and to leak useful information to the Allies. They had Canaris, who ran the Abwehr along similar lines. Above all they had Hitler, the corporal of World War I who regarded himself as a military genius, and who tended not to believe his intelligence services or his generals when they brought him information suggesting that his magnificent plans were flawed or failing.

One of Hitler's strikes, made for reasons that are not clear, brought about a battle that was fought without Ultra. It was the Battle of the Bulge, Germany's last counteroffensive. On December 16, 1944, Hitler launched an attack westward into Belgium, hoping to split the Allied armies that were advancing into Germany. Whether because he suspected that the Allies were reading the Enigma code, or wanted to make sure they didn't on this occasion, or believed (as he often said) that traitors were revealing his plans to the Allies, he imposed strict secrecy on the plans for the attack. One of his orders was that no messages about the attack were to be sent by radio. Ultra, you will recall, got all its information by intercepting and decoding German radio messages.

The result was that he took the Allies by surprise when he opened the attack at 5:30 A.M. on December 16. Although there had been some hints about it that other Allied intelligence channels might have picked up, the Allies had come to depend on Ultra. In its absence, they missed the hints. As the British official history of the war puts it, "The well-kept secret of what had been going on behind the German scene was largely undiscovered or misunderstood by Allied Intelligence and so not anticipated by Allied commanders." The Allies reeled backward from the attack and suffered heavy casualties before they were able to contain the German thrust and resume their advance into Germany.

But catastrophes like the Battle of the Bulge were rare after the first years of the war, largely because the Allies did have Ultra and Magic. A letter that Eisenhower sent to Menzies in July 1945 sums up the result. (Remember, he could not at that time use the word Ultra, so his references to it are veiled.) The letter read:

Dear General Menzies,

I had hoped to be able to pay a visit to Bletchley Park in order to thank you, Sir Edward Travis, and the members of the staff personally for the magnificent services which have been rendered to the Allied cause. I am very well aware of the immense amount of work and effort which has been involved in the production of the material with which you have supplied us. I fully realize also the numerous setbacks and difficulties with which you have had to contend and how you have always, by your supreme efforts, overcome them. The intelligence which has emanated from you before and during this campaign has been of priceless value to me. It has simplified my task as a commander enormously. It has saved thousands of British and American lives and, in no small way, contributed to the speed with which the enemy was routed and eventually forced to surrender. I should be grateful, therefore, if you would express to each and every one of those engaged in this work from me personally my heartfelt admiration and sincere thanks for their very decisive contribution to the Allied war effort.

Sincerely,
Dwight D. Eisenhower

***

Looking back over the intelligence activity in the war, one comes away with the impression that counterspies did better than spies. This was particularly true in England, where all or nearly all the German spies were found out and many of them were turned into double agents. In the United States, the FBI appears to have kept enemy spies in check. The record of Allied spies in Germany and Japan is thin.

Masterman thought about this situation when he summed up the double-cross operation after the war. He concluded that spying is hard and counterspying relatively easy in a war, whereas in time of peace "the boot is on the other foot." People in a country at war are on the lookout for spies, and the government usually runs a diligent counterespionage organization. In peacetime, however, people are not thinking much about spies. The peacetime counterespionage organization, if there is one, cannot simply arrest a suspected spy and either make him a double agent or imprison him. Instead, he must either be sent quietly out of the country or brought to trial in a court, where it is likely to be difficult to prove convincingly that what he was doing constituted spying.

Partly because spying can be productive in peacetime and partly because World War II showed how valuable it can be to monitor the communications of an enemy or a potential enemy, spying has been a big business since the war. The United States, which had no central intelligence organization before the war, now has the Central Intelligence Agency. It also has the National Security Agency, which monitors international communications. Both are large organizations. Their operations and their budgets are kept secret from the public but monitored by special committees of Congress. The Department of Defense also has extensive intelligence operations, including the Defense Intelligence Agency and individual intelligence groups in the army, navy and air force. Taken altogether, American intelligence organizations are thought to spend something like $30 billion a year.

In 1990, there was so much of this activity that many members of Congress were talking about reorganizing the intelligence apparatus to be more efficient and spend less. A report by the armed services committee of the House of Representatives put it this way: "The plethora of separate [intelligence] facilities, separate communications operations, separate data processing centers, separate training facilities, and separate support and warehousing operations is ripe for consolidation." Consolidation or not, however, it is certain that espionage and counterespionage will continue as major operations.

SUGGESTED READING

Brown, Anthony Cave. *Bodyguard of Lies*. New York: Harper & Row, 1975.

———. *The Last Hero*. New York: Times Books, 1982.

———. *"C"*. New York: Macmillan, 1987.

Buranelli, Vincent. *Spy/Counterspy*. New York: McGraw-Hill, 1982.

Calvocoressi, Peter. *Top Secret Ultra*. London: Cassell Ltd., 1980.

Casey, William. *The Secret War against Hitler*. Washington: Regnery Gateway, 1988.

Dulles, Allen. *The Secret Surrender*. New York: Harper & Row.

Goldston, Robert. *Sinister Touches*. New York: The Dial Press, 1982.

Hinsley, F. H. *British Intelligence in the Second World War*. New York: Cambridge University Press, 1979.

Knightley, Phillip. *The Second Oldest Profession*. New York: W. W. Norton & Company, 1986.

Lewin, Ronald. *Ultra Goes to War*. New York: McGraw-Hill, 1978.

———. *The Other Ultra*. London: Hutchinson & Co., 1982.

Lovell, Stanley P. *Of Spies and Strategems*. Englewood Cliffs, NJ: Prentice-Hall, 1963.

Masterman, J. C. *The Double-Cross System*. New Haven: Yale University Press, 1972.

Montagu, Ewen. *Beyond Top Secret Ultra*. New York: Coward, McCann & Geohegan, 1978.

Winterbotham, F. W. *The Ultra Secret*. New York: Harper & Row, 1974.

War Report of the OSS. Washington: U.S. Government Printing Office, 1949.

Index